I D E L L A

University Press of Florida
Florida A&M University, Tallahassee
Florida Atlantic University, Boca Raton
Florida Gulf Coast University, Ft. Myers
Florida International University, Miami
Florida State University, Tallahassee
New College of Florida, Sarasota
University of Central Florida, Orlando
University of Florida, Gainesville
University of North Florida, Jacksonville
University of South Florida, Tampa
University of West Florida, Pensacola

Idella Parker in the dining room at Van Hornesville, New York (1949).

I D E L L A

MARJORIE RAWLINGS'

" PERFECT MAID "

Idella Parker

with Mary Keating

University Press of Florida

Gainesville Tallahassee Tampa Boca Raton

Pensacola Orlando Miami Jacksonville

Ft. Myers Sarasota

24 23 22 21 20   8 7 6 5 4

Parker, Idella
Idella: Marjorie Rawlings' "perfect maid" / Idella Parker with Mary
Keating
p. cm.
Includes index.
ISBN 978-0-8130-1143-4 (cloth)
ISBN 978-0-8130-1144-8 (pbk.)
1. Rawlings, Marjorie Kinnan, 1896–1953—
Friends and associates.
2. Parker, Idella.
3. Women domestics—United States—Biography.
4. Authors, American—20th century—Biography.
I. Keating, Mary.   II. Title.
PS3535.A845Z84   1992
813'.52—dc20   92-8893
[B]

The University Press of Florida is the scholarly publishing agency
for the State University System of Florida, comprised of Florida
A&M University, Florida Atlantic University, Florida Gulf Coast
University, Florida International University, Florida State University, New College of Florida, University of Central Florida, University
of Florida, University of North Florida, University of South Florida,
University of West Florida.

University Press of Florida
2046 NE Waldo Road
Suite 2100
Gainesville, FL 32609
http://upress.ufl.edu

This book is dedicated to my sisters,
Hettie, Dorothy, Eliza, and Thelma,
and in loving memory of our brother, "E. M.",
and our beloved Mama and Papa.

C O N T E N T S

P R E F A C E

Marjorie Kinnan Rawlings called me "the perfect maid" in her book *Cross Creek*. Let me say right off that I am *not* perfect, and neither was Mrs. Rawlings, and this book will make that clear to anyone who reads it. It is the story of my life with Mrs. Rawlings, a story I have wanted to tell for a long time.

Mrs. Rawlings was one of the kindest persons I have ever known, but she could also be very hard to get along with and impossible to reason with at times. In other words, she was a human being, with human faults and troubles, and so am I.

From the beginning I was better educated than most of the help Mrs. Rawlings had, and it set me apart from some of the others. She told me that in all the years she lived out at Cross Creek, trying to write and plant and keep the groves going, I was the first helper who would let her work in peace.

Except for Mrs. Rawlings' husband, Norton Baskin, her friend Dessie Smith Prescott, and a few others, many of the people in this book are no longer living. I am not getting any younger myself, and I think young readers and students of Mrs. Rawlings' work have the right to know the truth as I saw it before I am gone, too. Truth is truth, and has a right to be written down, even though some of what I have to say is very painful to me.

Although every word in this book is true, it is not intended to be a scholarly work about Marjorie Rawlings. It is simply a collection of stories and anecdotes about Marjorie Rawlings and Idella Parker, their work and relationship, their friendship and disagreements, their times together. They are the recollections of a black woman who lived with, cared for, and struggled with a famous author. Some readers who are familiar with Marjorie Rawlings' letters will notice that sometimes my dates and her dates don't agree; I have tried not to use an exact date unless I am sure of it, and mine are all correct to the best of my memory.

Keep in mind as you read these stories that these things happened fifty years and more ago, before many of you younger readers were born. A lot has changed for me and for all black people since *Cross Creek* and *Cross Creek Cookery* were published, and I rejoice that I have lived long enough to see it happen. For one thing, we're not often called "Negroes" or "coloreds" or "niggers" now; we're African-Americans. I often wonder what's next! But because that is what we were called during the times I talk about, sometimes I use the old names in this book.

When she married Norton Baskin in 1941, Mrs. Rawlings asked me to start calling her Mrs. Baskin. I tried to do that, but sometimes the old habit of calling her Mrs. Rawlings caused me to slip. In this book I call her by both names, and I hope this will not confuse the reader.

If you visit the house at Cross Creek, you will find it very much as it was when I lived there with Mrs. Rawlings. Time has taken its toll, of course, and the house does not look as pretty or the grounds quite as perfectly kept as they were then. Freezes have killed off many of the orange trees that Mrs. Rawlings worked so hard to save, and the tenant house where I lived is not there any more. But the house is worth seeing, and in the fall of 1990 a new barn was erected to replace the one that was there when I first came.

They tell me that more people come to visit the Rawlings house at Cross Creek than any other state park in Florida, especially since the film *Cross Creek* appeared in 1983. Visitors come like pilgrims, to see the place that inspired Mrs. Rawlings to write so beautifully, and to imagine what life was like there.

I go there, too, and when I am there I remember Mrs. Rawlings and our times together. But Cross Creek does not fill me with longing for the "good old days." It stands as a reminder to me of how far we have come from those days of hard work and segregation. Cross Creek makes me grateful to be alive and to have seen all the changes that have come about for black people since I was young.

I said I was getting older, but please don't think that age has dimmed my lights. Like my father, whose mind was clear and whose memory was remarkable until his death at the age of 101, I remember clearly those years at Cross Creek. Every time I go there, I recall things that happened, stories that I have never told anyone, not even my family, until now. I remember every detail of how the house looked then, and what it was like to live out there. I can almost hear Mrs. Rawlings' footsteps on the wooden floors, and my ears listen for her voice or for the little bell she kept by the bedside to ring when I was needed.

So, enjoy your reading, and believe what I am about to tell you, for all of it is true, about both Marjorie Kinnan Rawlings and me, Idella, "the perfect maid."

ACKNOWLEDGMENTS

In 1976, just before I retired as a vocational teacher of home-making skills, I took a group of my students out to the house at Cross Creek, and ever since then, I have often been asked to come back to tell about my life out there. Many are the talks I have given to university groups, clubs, and schoolchildren. There is still a tremendous amount of interest in Marjorie Kinnan Rawlings and her works, and I am always surprised at how curious people are to know more about her. So I would like to thank the many people who asked me to write, because they convinced me that what I had to say would be of interest.

I enjoy telling about those days, because the youngsters in particular are always so amazed to hear how things were between the races back then. It may seem like ancient history to you of this generation, but it is true. These were the days of the Depression, when most black people were afraid of whites. I was one of those that feared. I think fear caused us to be obedient and do as we were told.

I say "told," because even Mrs. Rawlings, kind as she was, never asked her workers to do anything, she *told* them. In our first years together Mrs. Rawlings was just like other white people; she talked *at* me, not *to* me. Whatever she said do, I did.

As time went on, we became close friends, and I knew her as a kind, sensitive person who loved people and wanted to help anyone who was poor or needed help. I wish she had lived to see integration; I truly believe she would have welcomed it.

Much of the credit for restoring the house at Cross Creek must go to my good friend Sally Morrison, who worked tirelessly to return the house to the way it looked when Mrs. Rawlings lived there. Sally discovered who I was one day when I came to the house as a tourist, and from then on she welcomed me as a friend and advisor. I have been happy to help her and the people who worked there after she went on to other things, providing them with details about the house furnishings and how we did things. Sally has been a joy and an inspiration to me.

For years so many people have begged me to set down my memories of those years with Mrs. Rawlings. My cousin Dorothy Brown, a retired first-grade teacher, was with me the day Sally suggested I write a book. From that day on Dot kept after me to write, and in her gentle, insistent way she would not leave me alone until the work was done.

It was Dot who introduced me to her friend and fellow teacher at Reddick-Collier Elementary School, Mary Keating, and with their help the book finally was written. Dot opened her home in Reddick to us every Saturday morning and on countless evenings so that we'd have a quiet place to work, and Mary coaxed the stories out of me and got them down on paper, writing and rewriting until they were ready for publishing. I thank them both for their hard work and perseverance.

Sally, Dot, and Mary were not the first to suggest this book. Years ago Geri Anderson, a reporter from the Fort Lauderdale *Sun Sentinel,* came to my classroom at the Melrose Park Center. I was telling students that it's not the job itself, but how well you do that job that's important. I was talking about the types of jobs I had to do out at Cross Creek. I asked the students if they had seen the movie called *The Yearling,* and this caught their attention and caused them to sit up and listen. After class Ms. Anderson asked me why I didn't write a story about my life, and I have her to thank for the fact that from that day on I began to put down my memories, making notes and tapes against the day when I would get started.

Along the way, I have received a great deal of support and encouragement from Philip May, Jr., Professors Kevin McCarthy and Gordon Bigelow of the University of Florida, my friend Patricia Acton, Ginger Blinn and the other dedicated workers and volunteers at the Rawlings house in Cross Creek, and the many members of the Marjorie Kinnan Rawlings Society, each of whom has done a great deal to fan the flame of interest in everything connected with Marjorie Rawlings.

The Yearling is required reading in many Florida schools. A while back some seventh-grade students from the P. K. Yonge Laboratory School in Gainesville, who had just read the book, invited me to talk to them. We toured the house, cooked on the wood stove, and had lunch in the dining room.

They asked me dozens of questions, as young folks do, and as usual they were astonished to hear how different things were in those days before integration. I think by the time the afternoon was over, the students were beginning to understand how far society has come in fifty years.

But I couldn't help thinking that there are now whole generations who have grown up since those days and know very little about how things really were. That's when I made up my mind that it was time to begin writing, and this book is the result.

Marjorie Kinnan Rawlings and her dog Pat on the porch outside her bedroom at Cross Creek in the late 1930s.

" O N E "

Portrait of Mrs. Rawlings

To me, Marjorie Kinnan Rawlings was a lovely person, a woman I learned to love and care for through many years of joys and sorrows. Although I was black, and knew that I could only do or say just so much, we were more than servant and master. We were close friends and companions. She confided in me, and I have always kept her confidences. Even now that she is gone, there are many things about her I do not feel free to say.

What was she like? Mrs. Rawlings usually weighed about 180 pounds, and was about five foot seven inches tall. From the waist up she was small but bosomy, with very small hands and short, slim fingers. From the waist down she was heavy, with nice, well-shaped legs and the smallest feet. She must have worn a size three or four shoe. Her eyes were grayish blue. Her hair was unruly and she seldom gave any attention to it. She actually sent me to beauty school in Atlanta so that she wouldn't have to go to Ocala to have her hair fixed!

Mrs. Rawlings didn't care about how she looked. She was always clean, of course, but the types of dresses, shoes, and socks she sometimes put on would make me laugh. Most times around the house she wore socks, with pumps, sneakers, or long leather boots. I can see her now, climbing the stairs of the elegant Castle Warden hotel, wearing woolly white socks and black shoes with straps.

She always wore cotton dresses, the shirtwaist type, and most of them were blue, brown, or orchid in color. The skirts were always wide, because as I said, she was heavy from the waist down. When we were at the beach she wore culottes for her long walks, and often perched a beret on her head.

When Mrs. Rawlings was sure-enough dressed up you would find her in her one-piece black dress, always with a flared skirt. She had a winter and a summer black dress, usually covered with dog and cat hair. She never went anywhere without her bird dog, and in the house the cat was always all over her. She stayed covered with dog and cat hair, no matter how well the house was cleaned.

She loved hostess gowns, and she had many lovely ones to wear when she invited her higher friends. These were long flowing gowns, and they often seemed out of place for the occasion. When she went off to give talks or to travel, she wore tailored two-piece suits, usually topped by a little pillbox hat.

She pinned her hair back on both sides and wore bangs over her broad forehead. Her mouth was small, with very thin lips, and she seldom wore any makeup. Every once in a while she would put on a little lipstick.

She loved flowers, and always had something blooming in the garden wherever we lived. If there were no flowers in the garden, she would go into the woods and get a bouquet. Many times we stopped by the side of the highway to pick dandelions or wild lilies. This I always enjoyed with her. One or the other of us would sing out, "Oh, how pretty, look over there!" and we would stop the car and gather flowers to take home. It gave us both much joy. For me, it took my mind off what to fix for dinner or lunch, and I like to think that as she picked the flowers she must have been thinking of what to write next.

Mrs. Rawlings loved flowers, cats, and dogs; she loved the

outdoors and the woods. Each of her homes was far away from the crowd. Although she liked to entertain friends, most times she wanted to be alone. She loved to read, and she could read a book so fast! She had many books, and it seemed as fast as one came off the press she would get it from the bookstore in Gainesville or one would come in the mail, and she'd read it in no time at all. At times she would sit and read for hours: in bed leaning up against a backrest, or on the porch, any place it was quiet, smoking and reading, the dog down beside her, the cat crawling over her or asleep on the window ledge.

She loved to eat, and she enjoyed cooking as well as she enjoyed eating. She enjoyed having people eat her good food and ask questions about how this or that was fixed. This was when you could get a good grin out of her.

For the most part, she did not smile, and to me she seemed a lonely woman, no matter how many friends and admirers she had. She was always looking for happiness, only I don't think she ever really found it.

Mrs. Rawlings had a heart of gold. She loved poor people and did whatever she could to help those in need. But with all her lovely qualities, Marjorie Rawlings to me was a woman of more than one personality. This is the only way I can explain how a woman with so much talent and knowledge could have let herself fall into the habits she did.

She often drank far more than she should have, and she would fuss and cause a commotion when she had too much. She would cry readily, and often she knew that her conduct was wrong or unbecoming. She would smile up at me and say, "I will not get like this again. Come and help me up." I felt sorry for her, even when I had grown tired of hearing her always apologizing to me and to others for her behavior.

In our last years together, I tried daily to help her, tried to keep her from driving when she drank too much, tried to persuade her to put on another dress when she was going out and was not dressed well. But as time passed she became harder and harder to deal with, and her problems became too much for me to carry.

When at last I could not get her to listen to me, I had to leave. This happened not once but three times. Not long after I left her for the last time she died, and I felt a great sadness. I loved Mrs. Rawlings, but in my heart I knew that I had done all that I could for her.

I still keep in touch with Mr. Baskin. We talk on the telephone, and we remember the happy times and laugh about those days so long ago. He gave me his blessing on this book, but he asked me especially to be sure to tell about the good times as well as the bad times, and that is my intention. I want to begin at the beginning and tell you about me, my family, and how I came to work for Marjorie Kinnan Rawlings at Cross Creek. This is how it was.

My Early Years

When Marjorie Kinnan Rawlings drove into my yard in Reddick, Florida, on a hot, dusty September afternoon in 1940, I was expecting somebody else altogether. In fact, you might say I met Mrs. Rawlings and went to work for her at Cross Creek because of a mistake. But when something changes your life, the way meeting her changed mine, it's no mistake. It was most likely the good Lord looking out for me, and maybe looking out for her, too.

I was no stranger to work. By 1940, I'd been working for ten years, and giving all I earned to Mama to help the family out. Like most black families in those Depression days, we were poor and had to work hard for what we got. I remember people standing in line to get food, and how gasoline was rationed. We called them "Hoover days," or "hard times," and that's just what they were.

There were eight in our family: Papa, Mama, five daughters (I was the second), and one son. I was delivered at our house on

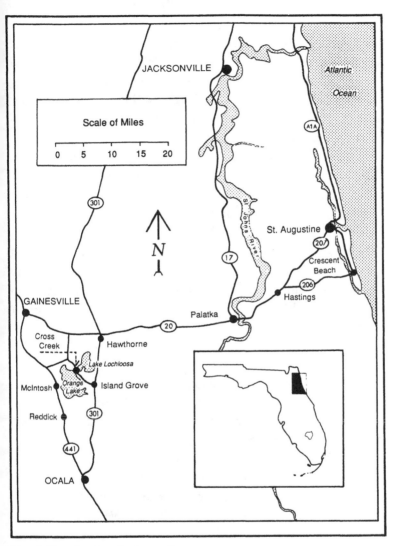

North Florida. Map by Janet Zugar.

Church Street one bright, sunny day in April 1914 by a midwife,
an old lady everyone called "Aunt" Hester Shannon.

As a youngster growing up I remember hearing people refer to
our little town of Reddick as a "one-horse town." I never could
understand the meaning of that statement, because there were

many, many horses in Reddick, and mules too! In the 1920s and '30s Reddick was a thriving farm community. We had a train depot with a telegraph office in it, and trains stopped regularly to pick up produce and passengers bound for Ocala or Gainesville. Near the depot there was a bank, a tiny limerock jail (or calaboose, as it was called), a boardinghouse, a doctor's office, a barber shop, and two meat markets.

Around the corner from the depot old Judge Cromartie held court on his front porch every Monday morning, deciding the fate of criminals in all manner of cases, from stealing chickens to stabbings and murder. You name the crime, and you could find it in our little town.

There were at least five dry goods and department stores, and one they called a "ladies' combination store." Here you could buy hats, dresses, shoes, and all types of ladies' wear. There were two churches in "white town," four churches on the black side of town, and three cemeteries.

There was a Masonic hall on one end of town and a nightclub, or "juke," known as Peter Brown's Hall on the other. Peter Brown divided his time among several jobs. He farmed, he ran his nightclub, and he was also the black school supervisor, riding his big red horse from school to school, making sure that all was in good order. If his schools were orderly, his nightclub surely was not, for it was here that many troubles would start. The sheriff's work was all cut out for him at Peter Brown's Hall.

Reddick always had its share of colorful characters, and one of the best known was my Uncle Adam Turner. We were related on my papa's side of the family. Papa's mother was called "Grandma Viney." Grandma Viney's father was Will Turner, and her uncle was Adam Turner. Adam and Will were brothers of the famous rebellious slave Nat Turner. I believe that makes Adam Turner my great-grand-uncle, but all my life everyone called him "Uncle Adam."

Nat Turner and his two brothers, Adam and Will, were slaves

from birth. Adam and Will were sold and brought to Florida by their master, and separated forever from Nat, who never came to Florida. As a child I remember Uncle Adam and Uncle Will talking about Captain Rou. They would reminisce about "Captain Rou's hill" or "Captain Rou's farm," and I think this may have been their master during slavery.

Uncle Adam would tell us about the slave days, and the children would sit at his feet with wide eyes, spellbound by his stories. He told how he and his brothers were field hands, while other slaves were house workers. How the bosses would ride on horseback through the fields with whips in their hands, ready to strike any slave who was not working hard enough or fast enough.

He told how Nat Turner always said that while he was working hard in the field he was working his brain hard, too, trying to think of a plan to set them all free. Out in the hot sun, all wet with sweat, they would send messages up and down the fields by singing, for they knew the bosses didn't mind them singing. The white overseers never understood the true import of these songs, and thought the slaves were just singing gospel songs. "Wade in the Water" signaled that work was being done in the escape tunnel—everybody keep watch. "Nobody Knows the Trouble I've Seen" meant that the white man was coming—danger. Sometimes they would sing "Couldn't Hear Nobody Pray" and sing it real loud, so if the overseers came close to the tunnel, the singing would cover the sound of hammers ringing.

Uncle Adam said this was the only way the slaves had to pass messages, and he would sing these songs in his quavery old voice and make the hair stand up on our heads. We could almost feel the danger. The way he looked, so wild, made the stories even more frightening to us.

Uncle Adam was a tiny brown-skinned man, only about five feet tall and no more than 120 pounds. I never saw him with shoes on. He had long, tangled white hair, bushy whiskers, and long, grey, unkempt mustaches. He was known for his wonderful intuition, and people called on him to interpret dreams and forecast the weather weeks in advance.

His hair was seldom combed. When he thought about combing it, he would gather about four of us children, sit down in his rocking chair, and hand us combs. We would crowd around him, all combing at once. When we pulled too hard, he would growl, "If you hurt me again, I am going to eat you up." We shook with fear, and believed that he ate children. Had you seen his wild appearance, you probably would have believed it yourself.

Uncle Adam owned what we call a half-section of land, or about 320 acres. He had a small one-room log cabin with a dirt floor, furnished with a rocking chair and an iron bed with a moss-stuffed mattress. There was a rock fireplace, and next to it were stacks of pine and oak firewood. I can still smell the sweet potatoes roasting on the fire, and hear the hissing of the old black kettle he always kept boiling.

The cabin had one door and two small windows, and Uncle Adam always knew what was going on outside. Near the cabin there was a large sinkhole, about fifty feet across, filled with water and surrounded by large oaks draped with Spanish moss. This was known as Uncle Adam's Pond, and its water was used for washing and for drinking. Next to the pond there was an orchard, which he also owned. This orchard was a great temptation to all the neighborhood children, who loved to try to snatch the peaches and plums.

Uncle Adam would almost always catch them. He would hobble out of his cabin and chase behind the screaming children, yelling, "You leave my plums. I'm going to eat you!" They would be so frightened there would be plums flying everywhere, dropped by terrified children.

Uncle Adam Turner died in 1929. He was 100 years old, fierce and independent to the end, and surely one of the most memorable characters I ever knew.

My papa, John Albert Thompson, was a share-cropper. Mind you, the white folks who owned the land had it pretty much figured out to where we didn't get much of a share, but it was the best we could do, so we took it and made the best of it. That's what we did in those days.

When he wasn't farming, Papa built wooden crates at the local citrus-packing sheds. There was nobody better or faster at making boxes than Papa. He could turn out one every minute, all day long, where other men could only build maybe two every five minutes. It was a skill Papa was proud of.

When there was no work around, Papa would have to leave home and find some. He worked every year of his life until 1980. That year he was ninety, and small and frail as he was, he could still build boxes faster and better than men a fraction of his age. If he hadn't been going blind, and his daughters hadn't insisted that he quit, I believe he'd have kept right on, the will to work was so strong in him.

When he was 96, we sat Papa down with a tape recorder and asked him to record some of the old stories he loved to tell. He talked on and on, his memory for dates and facts as sharp and clear as it had been all his life. After he died, at the age of 101, we wished we had asked him to record more stories and had not waited so long. How we cherish those tapes now.

Of all the fine qualities my sweet, kind papa had, the one I admired most was the pride he took in the hard work he did. I have said to young people time and again that they must do the very best they possibly can at any job they do, and they must have an attitude of pride in their work. I smile sometimes when I hear myself saying things like that, because it sounds just like Papa talking.

My mama stayed home and reared us children. Ethel Riley Thompson was without doubt the finest cook I have ever known, and she taught me all she knew. She always had a pot of something on the stove, and everybody in the neighborhood knew it. My cousin Dorothy Brown always tells people how she could never make the long walk home from school without stopping at Mama's for something to eat. Simple dishes like beans and rice, biscuits, and gingerbread tasted like nobody else's, and the house was full of warm, wonderful smells when Mama was cooking.

Mama was also a talented seamstress. All she had to do was look at a dress or blouse, and she could whip up one just like it in no time at all. Because of her skill, our family had nice clothes, and the house was filled with the many pretty things she made. She taught me everything I know about sewing, too.

Although she was good at many things, Mama had little formal schooling, yet she taught all her children that education was all-important. Because she made us so firm in that belief, all her children strove to get a good education and better themselves.

My sisters Thelma and Eliza became schoolteachers, Dorothy became a nurse, and Hettie was a teacher of nursing. My only brother, Edward Milton, called "E.M.," was studying to be a mortician before he was called into World War II and killed in action.

Schooling

To send a black child to school in those days cost money. Not much money, but often more than we had. One year, in order to pay the school fees, Mama pawned the only thing her own mother had left her, a gold piece. She got two dollars for it, enough to pay for school.

She had several months to pay the local pawnbroker back and reclaim the gold piece, but somehow she just never had enough money to do it. When she was finally able to scrape the two dollars together, the pawnbroker refused to take the money and wouldn't give the gold piece back.

I came home that day to find Mama standing at a window, staring out and crying. Mama was a big, strong woman who sel-

My mother, Ethel Riley Thompson (c. 1959).

dom cried, and it broke my heart to see her weeping so. She didn't want to tell me what was wrong, but I got the story of the gold piece out of her bit by bit. That's when I made up my mind to go to work and help out, so Mama would never have to cry like that again.

I got me a job within a week, washing dishes at Miss Alice Dupree's boardinghouse in Reddick. I was thirteen. Mama tried to talk me out of working so young, but I was as stubborn then as I am now. I made up my mind I was going to help out. I went to school whenever it was in session, I washed dishes too, and that's how it was.

Black children in our part of Florida didn't get much schooling back then. Our schools were only open three months of the year, because the children were needed to work in the fields, planting, hoeing, weeding, and picking the vegetables the families sharecropped. In those days children learned early what hard work was, and few of them ever went past eighth grade, because they had to work.

When school was open, black children walked, no matter how far away the school was or how bad the weather. My sisters and brother and I only had to walk two miles or so; others I knew walked eight miles or more. I thank God that things are better now than they were when I was a student.

I finished eighth grade at our local school, which was called Mount Zion, and I attended the Fessenden Academy in Martin for one year afterward. I was an A student, excelled at basketball and baseball, and I was often the teacher's helper. The following year, 1929, I was sent off to Daytona Beach to attend Bethune-Cookman, which was a high school in those days. Mrs. Mary McCleod Bethune, a remarkable lady who knew every child by name, ran the school with a rod of iron, tempered with love and understanding. I did well there, but I was sickly, and after a few months I had to be sent home.

I was quick at my lessons, and I loved to read. At home I made my three younger sisters and my brother play school, a game in which I was always the teacher. I began to think that I would like to teach young children, so I went up to Gainesville in 1929 and took the teacher's exam. There were three grades of certification, and I came away with a beginning teacher, or "third grade," certificate. I was sixteen.

For the next three years I taught in the black schools, one year in Levy County, the next in Marion County, a third year in

Hardee County. Every summer I returned to Bethune-Cookman to take a class and renew my teacher's certificate.

We were paid thirty dollars a month for three months of teaching. That was a lot of money in those days, but not enough to live on all year long. And, to tell the truth, the work was not what I thought it would be. We were watched carefully by supervisors like Peter Brown who rode from school to school on horseback. It seemed to me they meddled a lot more than they needed to, not only in the children's learning, but in the teachers' personal lives. They even went so far as to tell teachers where they could go after school hours, and where not. I decided teaching was not for me and did not return to it until many years later.

Finding Work

I was lucky to find work so close to home. In those days if there was no work, you had to go find some, or starve. It was common for black people to travel up and down Florida to find work. Some followed the crops, picking as the crops ripened. Others worked for rich white folks at the fancy seaside resorts.

Papa went to the resorts to work for several years. He would travel south to Fort Myers or Palmetto and work as a busboy during the winter season, then come back to Reddick to build boxes and sharecrop when the resort season was over.

I looked around for other work, but I couldn't find any near home, so in 1933 Mama let me travel to West Palm Beach with our friend and neighbor, Miss Rosa B. Heath. Miss Heath had a sister who ran a boardinghouse in West Palm Beach, catering to black workers from the resort hotels. The Heath sisters took in washing and ironing, and I worked with them for one season. It was hot, steamy work, but I loved being on my own in West Palm Beach, and I was proud to be able to send money home to Mama. But I knew I could find a much better job than that one.

The next season I went back to West Palm Beach, but this time I took a job with a nice white family, Mr. and Mrs. Owen Bowen.

13

I was cook and housekeeper to Mr. and Mrs. Bowen for five years, and they were wonderful to me. I loved West Palm Beach, loved being independent, and I had a fine room in a grand house to live in. I had many friends and an active church life there. It was a good life.

Under Mrs. Bowen's supervision I learned how to work for rich white folks. Mrs. Bowen was fond of having her lady friends in for fancy luncheons and teas, and soon I knew how to cook and serve all kinds of fancy dishes. Dainty sandwiches and fancy hors d'oeuvres, cheese souffles and rich desserts, I could do it all. I enjoyed cooking and took pride in serving food that looked as beautiful as it tasted.

For five years I went back and forth, going home to Reddick for visits with my family, and working in West Palm Beach. Unfortunately, this ideal working situation was ruined by a romance I had with a certain irresistible young man from Nassau by the name of Joe. He was handsome and fun, and he seemed wonderful at first, but in time Joe's attentions became abusive, and his presence in my life was disturbing. He began turning up at the Bowens' home and making scenes, so bad that after a while it was clear that the only way to get away from him was to leave West Palm Beach. Reluctantly, I left the Bowens and went home to Mama.

Once I was safely back in Reddick, I began to look for work. I let it be known around town that I was looking for a job and wanted to stay near home. The local grapevine, then as now, was working just fine. Pretty soon, Gary Neasman, a teacher at the Reddick school, told me his father knew of a cook position with the Camp family in Ocala.

The Camps were said to be quite wealthy, and Gary thought they'd pay a good salary. His father had been the Camps' chauffeur for years and always said the Camps were nice to work for. I got directions to find their house, and I could not wait. The very next day I asked a friend to drive me down to Ocala to see about the job.

"Is Mrs. Camp Home?"

When I got to the Camp house, there was nobody home, but I heard voices coming from a room over the garage at the back of the big house. I called out, and a tall, slim young man came out onto the landing at the top of the stairs.

I called up to him that I had come to ask about a job as cook for the Camps.

"My parents aren't home," he called back down to me. "They're in North Carolina, but they'll be back in two weeks. Come in and tell me how my mother can find you when she gets back."

So I climbed up to the door and told him my name, and how I had worked for the Bowens in West Palm Beach. I left out any mention of that troublesome devil Joe. I told young Mr. Camp how to find my home in Reddick, said my thanks, and turned to go.

As I went back down the stairs, I heard another person moving around inside the room. Later I learned that Mr. Camp's visitor was Cecil Clark. Both young men were friends of Norton Baskin, Mrs. Rawlings' future husband. Cecil Clark visited Cross Creek a few days later and told Mrs. Rawlings about me, but of course I didn't know anything about that.

Mrs. Camp Arrives, or So I Thought

On a hot September afternoon a few weeks later, I was sitting at home, expecting that Mrs. Camp would be back from North Carolina any time now, and I would be hearing from her. When a big two-door cream-colored Oldsmobile pulled into the yard and the horn tooted, the whole family came out on the unscreened porch to see who it was.

There was a white lady at the wheel, and a black and white bird dog in the back seat. She called out, "I'm looking for Idella Thompson."

I came down off the porch and walked up to the driver, a short woman with dark brown hair. I was wishing she had come at a better time. I was in the middle of straightening my hair, and half of it looked fine, but the other half was standing out in all directions.

She was smoking a cigarette, which she flicked out the car window every few seconds.

I said, "I'm Idella," and said it with a big smile, for I was sure this must be Mrs. Camp. I was also hoping the smile would take her attention off my sorry-looking hair!

She began talking very fast, the way I soon learned she spoke when she intended to get what she wanted.

"They tell me you're looking for work as a cook?"

I replied quickly, "Oh yes, ma'am."

"That's good. Can you cook?"

"Oh yes, ma'am, I'm a good cook." I was nodding enthusiastically now. By this time she had her checkbook out and was beginning to write quickly as she talked, asking me to spell my name.

As she wrote, she rattled on, fast as you please, "Now, I have to go up to New York and Maryland for a few weeks, but this check will bind us. Do you know where Island Grove is? Cross Creek is about five miles outside Island Grove."

By this time she had the check all made out, and she handed it to me. I looked at it and gave a start, because I saw that the name on the check was not Camp at all, it was Rawlings.

"Oh no, ma'am," I said in a loud voice, "I'm to work for Mrs. Camp. She lives in Ocala, not Island Grove." I tried to hand the check back to her, but she just waved it away.

I continued my protest, "But I'm to work in Ocala for Mrs. Camp."

Mrs. Rawlings looked up with a mischievous smile in her blue-gray eyes and said, "Oh no, Idella, you don't want to work for Mrs. Camp. She's hard to get along with."

With that she started to back the car up, and before I could say another word she waved and called, "Good-bye, I'll see you soon."

"Not Island Grove!"

The entire encounter had taken place so fast that I was literally dumbfounded. I walked slowly back to the porch, where my family was gathered to hear all about my interview with Mrs. Camp.

"Who was that woman, Idella? What did she want?" Mama asked.

I handed the check to her. It was made out for two dollars, but it might as well have been thousands for the weight it made me feel.

"Her name is Mrs. Rawlin's, Mama," I said, "and she wants me to work for her."

Suddenly it got real quiet, and I was almost afraid to say what came next.

"She says she lives not far from Island Grove."

Mama immediately got very upset, and her voice began to climb. "You just put that check up until that woman come back, and then you give that check right back to her." She was almost shouting now.

"You know you can't work in no Island Grove, child. They'll kill you!"

I knew what Mama was talking about. I'd been hearing stories about how sometimes colored folks mysteriously disappeared in Island Grove ever since I was a child, and those scary tales came rushing into my mind. Island Grove was a white man's town, a place where colored people were not welcome. We all feared Island Grove, that cold fear we all had of whites in those days. Mama was fearful for my safety, of what might happen to me if I so much as set foot in Island Grove. I was fearful of what might

17

happen if I didn't take the job after Mrs. Rawlings had paid me in advance.

In a week or so, I had a letter from Mrs. Rawlings, postmarked New York City and addressed to "Idella Thompson, Reddick, Florida." She wrote that she would be back soon, and she would drive down to get me on a certain day in October. I was to be packed and ready to go to Cross Creek. She enclosed another check for two dollars. Those checks seemed to seal my fate, so I made up my mind to go to Cross Creek, just to see what working there might be like. I would work four dollars' worth, then see.

I didn't fear Island Grove or Cross Creek as much as Mama did. Mama's fear was based mostly on the fact that she had no use whatsoever for white people. Any white woman who would take her baby off to Cross Creek was bad company as far as Mama was concerned. But when she suggested that I pack light in case I had to run off, I took her advice.

We got out an old footlocker, and the more Mama went on about how dangerous Island Grove was for a colored girl, the fewer clothes I packed. I put in the two gray maid's uniforms I had worn in West Palm Beach, a white apron and a stiff little white cap to complete the uniform, some underwear, a nightie, and a sweater. That's all there was in that big old box, for in my mind I was thinking I might have to leave in a hurry.

Driving to Cross Creek

On the October afternoon set by Mrs. Rawlings, I got dressed in a flowered cotton dress and my best brown and white oxfords and sat down on the front porch to wait for her. I was packed and ready to go to Cross Creek.

When she drove into the yard, Mrs. Rawlings had the same passenger in the back seat, a medium-sized black and white spotted bird dog she called Pat. I loaded my suspiciously light footlocker into the trunk and was faced with the problem of Pat. As I opened the passenger door and leaned the front seat up to sit in the back, the way black people were expected to do in those days, I could see that Pat thought it was his seat. He was walking back and forth on it, lolling his tongue out, wagging his tail happily, and drooling all over the place. There was dog hair everywhere. Mrs. Rawlings seemed to sense my hesitation and said, very matter-of-fact, "Sit in the front, Idella. Always sit in front with me."

I must have looked surprised, because she had to urge me to get in so we could go. To tell the truth, I was more than surprised. Remember this was 1940, in the days when we were known as "colored people," "Negroes," or just plain "niggers." Wherever you went in those days you'd see signs: WHITES ONLY.

We weren't allowed to register, so we couldn't vote. We didn't enter white people's houses by the front door, and we were taught to address white people with "yes, sir" and "no, ma'am," not just "yes" or "no." We sat in the back seats on public buses and separate cars on trains, and we *sure* didn't sit up front in a white lady's car. That's just how it was. And here was a white lady I didn't really know, telling me to sit up front with her like it was an everyday thing. I didn't know what to think of her, but I did as she said.

I don't recall that we talked very much on the drive north to Cross Creek. I sat quietly, nervous and scrunched way over close to the door with my hands in my lap, and had a good look at this white lady I was going to work for.

She had brown hair, worn very plain, pulled back from her face and pinned, with one side arranged down across her forehead. Her face was broad, and she wore no makeup. I was astonished that she seemed to have very thin lips, almost no lips at all. She had a nice figure, with a full bosom, and was wearing one of the cotton shirtwaist dresses I would find out she favored. She had small hands and tiny fingers, and the smallest feet I think I have ever seen on a woman.

When she spoke, she spoke fast, the words sort of tumbling

out. She smoked as she drove, flicking the ashes out the window more often than she needed to.

I think we talked about the weather and such things. I noticed some beautiful white flowers, and she told me their name. I was keeping one eye on the road and the other on the speedometer, because she was driving fast and swerving every time she looked over at me, making it hard to keep my mind on small talk.

It was not much of a conversation, but by the time we turned west from Island Grove and headed down the unpaved road to Cross Creek, I was feeling more at ease and was beginning to like her. She was nice.

After we passed the filling station and the few houses at Island Grove, there was nothing but a line of towering live oak trees on either side of a narrow, sandy road. It seemed like a long ride, but it was beautiful. Huge, dark magnolias were in full, fragrant white bloom; the palm trees and palmettos scattered among the live oaks and covered with vines were a lovely sight to see.

At last Mrs. Rawlings slowed down and turned left, and the car bumped across a cattle guard and into a curving driveway lined on both sides with the biggest, most beautiful white spider lilies I have ever seen. As the car rolled into the yard, I saw grass as green and carefully tended as any fancy golf course and a profusion of flowers planted all around the house. The house was white with green trim, nothing fancy, but with a neat and well-kept look about it.

There were pecan trees loaded with nuts, and orange, grapefruit, and tangerine trees all over the yard, each one heavy with fruit. Circling this wonderful yard there were woods, dark and tangled as the ones we had passed on the road. It was like discovering a magic garden in the midst of a jungle.

As we came to a stop under the carport, I couldn't help blurting out, "Oh my Lord, how pretty!"

This must have been the first time Mrs. Rawlings had ever heard a black person express so much enthusiasm over her place,

A side view of Marjorie Kinnan Rawlings' house at Cross Creek; the front porch is at the right of the picture. Courtesy of the Rawlings Collection, Rare Books and Manuscripts, University of Florida Libraries.

because the look on her face was one of genuine surprise. She turned, took the cigarette out of her mouth, and her blue-gray eyes got very wide.

"Idella, do you like it?"

I got out of the car, and for a few minutes we just stood there in the yard together, looking around and smiling.

I'll never forget the sky that evening. I can still see it today. The sun was just about to set, huge and red in the sky. The clouds were puffy, some white, others blue, and the white ones seemed to be chasing the blue ones across the sky until they all hid behind some orange trees.

"Oh my," I exclaimed, "what a sight to behold."

Suddenly, Mrs. Rawlings turned her head eastward, and broke the mood with an ear-splitting "Yoo-hoo." Within a few minutes, what seemed like a whole lot of black people came running up from out of the woods. They crowded around us, and Mrs. Rawlings introduced them to me.

There was old Mrs. Martha Mickens, tall and thin, with a large hooked nose, a bandanna around her gray hair, and a huge white apron over her dress. She nodded, smiling, and said, "How you doin', Sugar?" She called everybody "Sugar" or "Honey."

There was Martha's son, Little Will, a big strong young man dressed in overalls, and Little Will's girlfriend, Alberta, shy and barefooted. As I said hello, I felt a cat rubbing himself all around my legs, and I couldn't move without tripping over him. This was Mrs. Rawlings' Siamese, Smokey. Meanwhile the dog, Pat, had to get some attention now that he had jumped out of the car, so he proceeded to show me that he could open the screen door that led to the kitchen.

"Can you beat that?" I laughed. "That dog can open the door!"

Pat looked back at us and rolled his eyes. Everybody laughed, and I remember thinking, *What a bunch!*

It was beginning to get dark, so Mrs. Rawlings told Martha to take me to my room, and said that in the morning Martha would show me what to do in the house. She smiled, said good-night, and went on into the house.

Little Will shouldered my footlocker, and Martha led the way down a wooded path to a little unpainted wood frame house I hadn't seen when we drove in. This was where the Mickens family lived, and they called it the "tenant house." It was small, with two tiny bedrooms and a small living and kitchen area. The outhouse we all used was out behind the tenant house, hidden by some trees at the edge of an orange grove, and a number 2 tin

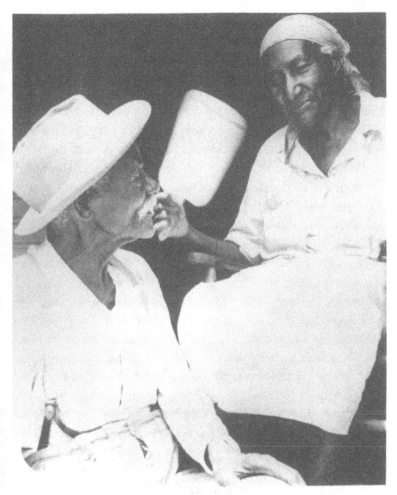

Will and Martha Mickens. Courtesy of the Rawlings Collection, Rare Books and Manuscripts, University of Florida Libraries.

washtub hanging on a nail outside the tenant house was our bathtub.

We climbed the stairs of the tiny unscreened front porch, and Martha introduced me to her husband, Will, who was sitting tipped back in a chair with his feet up on the porch rail. He had white, silky, straight hair, and a long white mustache, nicely trimmed. Even in overalls he was dapper.

Now this man was some character, and I soon learned that the porch was where he always sat, because from this vantage point he could watch all the comings and goings at the main house. There he sat, watching and commenting on everybody's business at Cross Creek. As far as I ever saw, he did exactly nothing from one day to the next, and never had anything nice to say about anybody. He sat with his feet up on the railing of the tenant house porch all day, saw everything and everyone who passed, and knew what everyone was doing at the Creek. He would stroll down the road almost daily to Mr. Brice's house. Will called him Old Boss, and said, yes, Old Boss had always ruled the Creek.

Then along came Mrs. Rawlings, who, Will said, also wanted to rule the Creek, and he declared that that was when the feuding began, for each of these rich people wanted to be the ruler. How it ended, you can guess, for when Mrs. Rawlings lit a cigarette and showed those catlike eyes, and almost every other word was a curse, well, everyone would listen. Whatever Mrs. Rawlings said or did was right, or you had better say it was right. What a woman she was!

Will called Mrs. Rawlings "Old Miss" behind her back, and she couldn't stand him. But she was afraid that if she ran Will off, his wife Martha would follow him. He greeted me right off with, "How you doin', Cook?", and ever after that's what he called me.

Martha led me in the front door to my room. It was a tiny room, with no decorations at all. No curtains, no pictures on the wall, nothing but a curtain strung across the door that led to the other bedroom, where the entire Mickens family slept. My bed was an army cot, and for furniture there was a straight chair, a small potbelly stove, a kerosene lamp on a small table, a pitcher and bowl to wash up in, and a chamber pot.

After Martha said good-night, I washed myself, hung my uniforms up on nails in the wall, and lay down on the cot to think and pray: *Lord, what kind of place is this?* I had had a much nicer place at the Bowens' house in West Palm Beach. Even at home, poor as my family was, we had more privacy than a curtain on a string across a door. And an army cot for a bed?

I was disturbed by the living arrangements, and surprised that a rich lady like Mrs. Rawlings would provide her help with so few comforts. I guess I was also feeling sorry for myself. I never said any of these things out loud to anybody, of course. I just kept my feelings to myself and prayed on it.

On second thought, it came to me that I was being treated as a privileged person, having a room to myself when the whole Mickens family had to share. And Mrs. Rawlings was not really what you could call rich at that time. She was what I would call stepping up from poor to rich. But I didn't know these things that first night at Cross Creek. All I knew was that this was beginning to look like a rough place to work. I put out the lamp and wondered what I had got myself into and what the morning would bring.

The way I felt that first night, it's a wonder I stayed. I never dreamed that I would be there ten years, or that I would come to love Cross Creek almost as much as Mrs. Rawlings did.

" T W O "

Work Begins

Martha woke me before six next morning, saying, "Sugar, let's get up to the house, for Mrs. Rawlin's have her breakfast at seven each mornin'."

I dressed in my gray uniform, apron, and cap, and we left the tenant house in a hurry, Martha leading the way and me practically running to keep up with her big strides. We went into the house by the kitchen door, and Martha set about getting a fire going in the big wood stove.

Once the fire was going good, she got out a big enamel coffee pot, put in the coffee and water, and set it on to boil. Next she crushed an eggshell and put it in the pot, to settle the coffee, she explained. She put one egg in a small pot to boil, and when I asked how long it should cook she said vaguely, "Oh, you just let it boil a while, is all." I guessed from this that Mrs. Rawlings really *did* need a cook.

Next we cut and squeezed enough fresh oranges for a tall glass of juice, and Martha got out a large silver tray and began setting the breakfast dishes in place. As we worked Martha told me just how "Missy," as she called her, liked her breakfast tray.

There had to be a fresh flower in a small silver vase, placed at

27

the top right-hand corner of the tray. At the top center, a silver coffee pot and the sugar and creamer. The egg cup and juice would go in the lower center of the tray, with a linen napkin and silverware to the left. At the top left corner, a small bowl of milk and a dish of canned cat food for Smokey. I would find that the time and the menu never varied, except that every so often Mrs. Rawlings would ask for toast.

Once we had everything ready, I picked up the tray and followed Martha to the bedroom. Mrs. Rawlings was already awake and greeted us with a smile and some pleasant words. Martha fluffed up the bed pillows, and I placed the tray down on the bed in front of her.

Smokey leisurely stretched, yawned, and walked across the bed and began eating his breakfast right off the tray. I had never in all my days seen a cat eat off the same tray as a human, but I kept my amazement to myself and tried not to look surprised. Pat was curled up in the armchair, not the least bit interested in breakfast. He was fed in the evening and seemed to know this meal was not for him.

The morning was chilly, so Martha started a fire in the small bedroom fireplace. I wondered why the fire wasn't lit before making breakfast, but I guessed that was how they did things at Cross Creek, so I never questioned it.

For months afterward I prepared the breakfast tray exactly as Martha showed me that first morning, and lit the fire when I took the breakfast tray in. I never questioned the way anything was done, I just did as I was told. It was many months before I felt comfortable and confident enough to begin making small changes of my own in the routines of the house.

The Daily Routine

When she was done with the breakfast tray, Mrs. Rawlings would call us by ringing a little bell she had by the bed. By the time I had the dishes washed and put away, she would be dressed and gone from the bedroom, either into the front part of the house or out into the garden to pick fresh flowers.

Martha took me back to the bedroom to show me how to make up the bed. It was a beautiful bed, with lace embroidered pillowcases, fancy sheets and quilts, and a fluffy white and brown fur rug lying on the floor. Mrs. Rawlings loved pretty bed linens, and kept a variety of them on hand.

As Martha showed me around the rest of the house, I noticed dust, cobwebs, and animal fur everywhere. I decided I would soon put that to rights, even though Martha told me that after the breakfast dishes were done and the table was scrubbed down, all I had to do was sit and wait in case I was needed. I've never been good at just sitting, but the first week or so I did as Martha said, so the job was easy.

I always had great respect for Martha, or "Miss Martha," as I called her. She was kind to me, and she was a hard, hard worker. She was Mrs. Rawlings' pet, her "heartstrings." She had been with Mrs. Rawlings for so many years that she had a sixth sense about when she would be needed. When she was down at the tenant house, she always kept one eye on the main house.

From the front porch of the tenant house she could see straight across to the house, and she would come running any-time Mrs. Rawlings called, sometimes even before she called.

She would say, "Sugar, I'm just here to take up the slack for Missy," and she did that and much more.

Every morning Martha's son, Little Will, appeared at the side door with a bucket of milk fresh from the cow, Dora. Martha would always meet him at the door and take the bucket from him. I soon understood that Will never came in the house, except to fill the woodbox on the porch, and even then Martha was there to oversee him. Will's work was outdoors, as was his girlfriend, Alberta's. She tended to the garden and the chickens, and sometimes helped with laundry on wash day.

Outside the back porch at Cross Creek (c. 1941). I'm on the back step carrying a bucket, Little Will Mickens is carrying firewood, his girlfriend, Alberta, is at the pump, and Martha Mickens is holding a bucket under the pump. Courtesy of the Rawlings Collection, Rare Books and Manuscripts, University of Florida Libraries.

As the weeks went by, I began to see why Martha kept such a close eye on her son. Little Will sipped at a whiskey bottle all day long, and stayed pretty well drunk all the time. Martha managed to cover up this fact in such a way that Mrs. Rawlings didn't know about it, or at least wasn't troubled by it. She did this by watching him constantly and keeping him well away from the house.

Occasionally, Little Will would go out "jukin'" on a weekend and not come back on Monday. When this happened, Martha would jump right in and take up the slack for him too, doing his jobs. She loved her baby, and did whatever it took to protect him.

One of Martha's jobs was to see to the milk every day. She strained the fresh milk into special pans and put them on the white enamel table in the kitchen. Then she would take yesterday's milk out of the icebox and skim off the thickest buttercup-yellow cream you ever saw. If you have read *Cross Creek* or *Cross Creek Cookery*, you know that we used heavy cream in many dishes, as well as in coffee. I'm not sure what Dora was given to eat, but whatever it was, I have never since seen such rich cream as she gave us daily.

Every so often Martha would churn butter. These were always her jobs, taking care of the milk, cream, and butter. Sometimes poorer neighbors, including Martha's daughter Sissie, would come to the kitchen door with a bucket, and Martha always gave them milk to take home. Dora gave us much more than our little household could use.

The icebox was outside the kitchen on the side porch, and as the name says, had a big chunk of ice inside it to keep the food cool. Blocks of ice were delivered every day by a man from Hawthorne, and the melted water had to be emptied out every day, too. Young people, you don't know what hard work is until you have kept house and cooked as we did those days at Cross Creek.

The way we had to do laundry, for instance. I thank God every day for the blessing of a washing machine and dryer. Back in those days at Cross Creek, laundry day started early, when Little Will started a wood fire in the side yard and set a big black laundry pot on to boil. He would pump all the water for us, and it took many and many a tubful to do the wash, all drawn by hand with the pump outside the kitchen door.

Martha would sort the clothes into piles, same as people do today: white, colored, dark, and so on. Then she would wet the clothes down in number 2 tin washtubs full of cold water, and she would get out the homemade lye soap, or sometimes a bar of storebought Octagon laundry soap. She would commence to scrub those clothes on a washboard, paying special attention to spots.

Once the clothes were scrubbed, she would put them in the pot of boiling water and "chuke" them down (poke them) with a wooden pole. This had to be done often so the clothes wouldn't scorch at the bottom of the pot.

After they had boiled thirty or forty minutes, Martha hauled the hot, heavy clothes out with a pole and put them in washtubs full of clear cold water and rinsed them twice. Then they were wrung out, shaken, and put up on the clothesline to dry. Alberta would drop her garden hoe and come over to help hang up the sheets and linens, and if I was free I would help too.

In the late afternoon Martha would take down the dry clothes and fold them neatly for ironing the next day. They always smelled so fresh and clean dried in the open air. It's a wonderful smell, one you just don't get from a dryer.

Next day, between meals and other duties, we would iron. The iron was heated on the wood stove or in the dining room fireplace if it was going, and an ironing board covered with a white sheet was placed between two chairs. We sprinkled and ironed everything in those days, including sheets. Thanks to drip-dry, no-iron, and polyester fabrics, not much is ironed these days, and life is a lot easier.

Although I had been hired at Cross Creek to cook, I helped Martha with the washing and ironing, scrubbed floors on my hands and knees, polished silver, and did many of the thousand jobs it took to keep a house nice, almost all of them by hand. When I tell young people about the work, how hard it was, they find it hard to believe, but it was true. This isn't ancient history, young readers. This was only fifty years ago.

We had little time to talk or socialize; there was something to do all day long, and the day lasted from dawn till cleanup after supper, later if we had dinner guests. On company nights it was often midnight or later before I could rest my weary head. When

I tell you that you don't know what hard work is until you've kept house like we did, I know what I'm talking about.

"Mrs. Rawlin's is a Writer!"

It was rough work, but I liked it. I liked the quiet of the Creek, the birds singing all day, the beautiful garden I could see out the kitchen windows. I liked Mrs. Rawlings, who kept coming out to the kitchen to ask how I was doing, was I finding everything, did I like my work. Although she told me Martha would see to me, she took time out from her work many times those first few weeks to talk to me, show me where things were, and tell me how she wanted things done.

The large, screened-in front porch was her favorite place in the house, and most days she asked for her lunch to be served out there. Those first few days I would see her there all morning, reading or looking out at what she called "the young grove" of orange trees. Sometimes she would be sitting at a typewriter typing away, but it was many weeks before I discovered Mrs. Rawlings was a writer.

One day, tired of sitting and doing nothing as Martha had told me to do, I took a duster and went into the living room to dust the books in the bookcase. They had not been dusted for a long time, I could see that. As I dusted, I took out one book after another and, because I loved to read, I opened one up and soon became lost in it.

I did not hear Mrs. Rawlings come up behind me, and my heart almost stopped when I heard her say, "Good morning!"

"Good morning," I answered, and quickly put the book away. *First week at work*, I thought, *and here she's caught me not working.*

I was expecting a scolding, but instead she said, "Idella, do you like to read?" She seemed surprised, because in those days not many black people could read.

But I told her yes, I liked to read, and would she mind if I borrowed a book from time to time to read at night.

"Why yes, of course you can," she said warmly. "Just let me know which one you've taken." Then she added, "Have you ever seen any of my books?"

I was astonished! Up until then I hadn't known what she did to earn a living. (I knew that her ex-husband was a writer, because she mentioned to me that he wrote articles for the *Saturday Evening Post.* She never did say anything more about him to me.)

"No, ma'am, Mrs. Rawlin's," I stammered. "I didn't know you wrote books."

"Oh yes, Idella, that's what I do," she laughed, and began to show me copies of some of her works. That day she loaned me one to read; *Golden Apples,* I think it was.

Another day I went out on the porch and started to straighten up the mess of papers on the porch table, and pick up some of the wadded-up papers she had thrown on the floor. She always wrote on long yellow legal tablets, and there were yellow paper balls thrown everywhere.

"Oh no, Idella, don't ever touch anything on this table or anywhere around it," she said. "I know it's a mess, but you just leave it alone, and I'll take care of it."

As the first months went by, I began to see that working for a writer was not like working for some other folks. It meant staying out of the way when she was working, and trying to be quiet so she could concentrate. It meant learning that some days the work went well and she would be in a happy mood. Other days, nothing went right and she could be in a very dark mood indeed. It meant taking the burden of running a house off her shoulders, and that's what I tried to do.

Within a few months she was telling me the problems she'd had keeping good help. Martha's daughter Adrenna had been cook before me. To hear Mrs. Rawlings tell it, Adrenna cared more about running after men than working. When Adrenna came back to Cross Creek some months after I came, with a fair-skinned baby, Mrs. Rawlings refused to take her back.

Then there was 'Geechee, whose name described the dialect she spoke. She had also been Mrs. Rawlings' cook, and was mentioned in *Cross Creek*. 'Geechee surprised us with visits to Cross Creek on two different occasions while I was there. The first time she walked up to the kitchen door and asked to see Mrs. Rawlings. By then one of my jobs was to keep people away when Mrs. Rawlings was writing, but she must have heard our conversation at the back door.

Here she came running, thump, thump, thump, calling, "'Geechee? 'Geechee? Is that you?"

They had a joyful reunion, hugging and carrying on about how good it was to see one another. Mrs. Rawlings took 'Geechee out to the front porch, where they sat and talked a short while. I worried some that maybe 'Geechee wanted to come back, but nothing ever came of either of these visits, and I can't say whether 'Geechee came looking for work or just wanted to visit with her old boss.

There had been other workers before me too, none very good. She said she was always having to leave her work when her helpers came in with this or that problem. I had sense enough not to bother her when she was working, and I know she appreciated that.

Settling In

Those first weeks, as I learned what to do, I gradually became more independent, and before long Martha did not need to show me very much. I began to show off some of the cooking skills I had.

I never slapped things on a plate to serve to Mrs. Rawlings, but always took time to do fancy things. I'd arrange the plates nicely, and add touches of garnish, such as fresh herbs from the garden. If a tomato was served, it might be carved in the shape of

Martha Mickens (left) and me (right), cooking for a dinner party at Cross Creek (c. 1939–40). Courtesy of the Rawlings Collection, Rare Books and Manuscripts, University of Florida Libraries.

a flower and maybe some fancy filling added. These little touches pleased Mrs. Rawlings very much, and she always said so.

Soon she was coming to the kitchen every day to talk over what we should have for lunch or dinner, what supplies were needed, and asking me to tell her some of my recipes (all of which were in my head and hands, but not written down). She would ask me whether I knew how to cook this dish or that, and was always delighted when I said yes, I could.

Little by little, the house began to shine. I made it my business to dust, clean, scrub, and polish whenever I had time between meals and other chores. And little by little Mrs. Rawlings began to relax and enjoy having things done without having to say much.

Soon she began to brag about me, first in the house, saying things like, "I think Idella is going to stay." Then she said it to friends and visitors, in her letters, and even in her book *Cross Creek*. She called me "the perfect maid," which makes me smile, for I am no more perfect than anybody else. But I knew how to do things, knew how to cook well, and I like to think I made her life and her writing a little easier for her. To her I was perfect because I knew what to do without being told, and because I eased her mind.

One week I went home to visit Mama in Reddick, and I sewed up some little yellow gingham curtains for the kitchen at Cross Creek. Mrs. Rawlings was tickled.

"Yes," she declared, "I do believe Idella is going to stay."

Soon after the curtains went up, Mrs. Rawlings drove into Ocala without a word to me. She went to the Eagle Furniture Store and had them deliver to the tenant house a nice double bed with a good mattress and spring, a chest of drawers, a large mirror, and a comfortable flowered armchair, all for me.

Then she had a carpenter come out and put a real door with a lock on it between my bedroom and the Mickens'. She screened in the tenant house porch and put a porch swing on it, big enough to hold three people. My, we were some happy people to see all these improvements, for now all of us could rest comfortably after our day's work.

Once this nice new furniture was in place I felt at home, and knew that I was there to stay.

Nothing made Mrs. Rawlings happier than to find out I could drive. One morning, several months after I had come to Cross Creek, I carried the breakfast tray in and right away I knew something was wrong. Mrs. Rawlings was in bed shaking and shivering, with the covers pulled up around her face. She tossed and turned and moaned, and I could see her face looked all red.

"What's wrong, Mrs. Rawlin's? What's the matter?" I cried.

"Oh Idella, what am I going to do? Miss Julia's coming." (Miss Julia was Julia Scribner, the daughter of Mrs. Rawlings' publisher, and one of her closest friends.)

"Miss Julia's coming, and I'm so sick. I can't drive to Gainesville to get her. And I'll be *damned* if I'm going to let Will drive my car. And I don't want him to pick Julia up in that old truck. Oh, what in the world am I going to do?"

"Well, I'll go get her," I said without thinking. "I can drive your car."

"Idella, you can drive?" She sat up in bed like she had an electric shock. "You really can drive, you have a license?"

"Yes, ma'am."

"Let me see it, where is it, go get it." She was talking fast, and I knew what that meant. So off I ran to the tenant house, got my driver's license, and came running back with it, all out of breath, and showed it to her.

"Why, Idella, I never dreamed you could drive, that's wonderful," she sighed, and settled back down on her pillows. "You take my car and go to the train station in Gainesville, and meet Miss Julia's train."

"But, Mrs. Rawlin's," I said, "I don't know what Miss Julia looks like, how will I know which one she is?"

"You just stand on the platform when the people are getting off, and yell out 'Miss Julia.' She'll hear you," was the reply.

I always obeyed her, so that's exactly what I did. I drove that big Oldsmobile to Gainesville, and took my place on the platform in time for Miss Julia's train. My heart sank when I saw there were dozens of passengers getting off in Gainesville that day, but I did just what I was told. I stood there yelling "Miss Julia, Miss Julia" at the top of my voice, and I don't need to tell you I got many curious looks.

Finally a sophisticated young woman with close-cropped blonde hair got off the train, and said, "I'm Julia," and I was saved from further embarrassment. She wore a double-breasted tweed pants suit, and she looked like a college student, so young. (I wondered that Mrs. Rawlings, who seemed much older than this woman, called her her best friend. It turned out that she was kind of like the daughter that Mrs. Rawlings never had.)

"Mrs. Rawlin's sent me to get you," I said. "I'm Idella."

"Marge? Where's Marge?" Miss Julia was immediately concerned.

"Mrs. Rawlin's is sick," I replied, "but she says she'll be up and around in a day or so." So I got Miss Julia's bags, and we headed back down Route 20 to Cross Creek.

When we got to the house, Miss Julia ran straight to Mrs. Rawlings' room, real anxious about her.

"Marge, are you all right?" she cried.

"It's just a virus," came the reply from the bed. "Don't worry, I'll be fine in a day or so. You've met Idella. Idella saved me today by going to get you." I smiled and was pleased.

From that day on Mrs. Rawlings' car was my car, and she relied on me to do most of the driving. It was a good thing, too, because Mrs. Rawlings was not a good driver. The speed limit on open highways in those days was 70, but she paid little attention to that. To tell the truth, I always felt safer when I drove.

Many years later, recalling this incident, I thought to myself, now why didn't we make a sign with Miss Julia's name on it, and I could have held it up, and not had to yell like that? But at the time it never occurred to me to question anything I was told to do. That's just how things were.

Julia Scribner came to visit many times after that, and she was a very nice young lady. I was always pleased when Mrs. Rawlings would tell me that we were going to have a visit from Miss Julia.

Sundays Off

There were very few times I didn't do as Mrs. Rawlings said to do, but one of those times came on a Sunday morning when I had been at the Creek for almost three months, and had never yet had a day off. She did drop me off at Mama's house in Reddick every once in a while to visit for a few hours while she drove into Ocala on errands. But I had not yet had a real day off, away from Cross Creek. I was free on Sunday afternoon, but there was nothing to do out there, no place to go, so I just sat around. I was wanting to go to church, and see my family, but there was no way to get there.

I thought to myself, "This must be what working on a plantation was like." It seemed just like what my grandmother had told me about slavery. All the days I had been there, all I saw was Mrs. Rawlings and the people who worked for her. From six in the morning until dark every day we worked. We spent no time talking, unless it was talk about what we were doing, or what was to be done next.

There was no social life for me there at the Creek at all, because the other workers and I had very little in common. I didn't enjoy "jukin'," and there was no church for me to belong to nearby. Including Mrs. Rawlings' house there were only five houses in Cross Creek, all owned by white people. There were no churches, no stores, no telephones, and no transportation except what was provided by Mrs. Rawlings. The nearest town was five miles away, and you didn't dare try to walk. Few cars passed, and all manner of snakes were always crawling across the road, so you were afraid. I felt like I was stuck in Cross Creek.

This particular Sunday, I was determined not to work. In fact, I was thinking it might be about time to go back home to Mama.

Mrs. Rawlings came out and set down a blue dress and told me to hem it for her while she showered.

When she got out of the shower, she called, "Idella, did you finish?" I said, "No, ma'am, I didn't finish," and then I told her just how I felt about being locked up at Cross Creek for so long.

"Mrs. Rawlin's, I work out here for you six days and nights, and you wait till Sunday to ask me to hem a dress. I can't go to church. I got no way to go anywhere, but it's Sunday, and I am *not* going to sew no dress."

I knew she was furious. Her face turned bright red. She was so mad she didn't know *what* to do. She snatched up the dress and stomped back to her room. After a while she came back out and threw her car keys at me and cursed me real good. My, how that woman could curse!

"You go to any ***** church you like!" she shouted, and stomped off again, her heavy footsteps shaking the little house in her anger.

But I left the keys alone and spent that Sunday in my room as usual, alone. It was a long Sunday.

By Monday, she had calmed down, and she came to me and apologized.

"I didn't know you wanted to go to church, Idella. From now on, unless I have company—and I'll always let you know if there is going to be company—you just leave me something I can eat, take the car, and go to church."

And from that day, that's the arrangement we had.

" T H R E E "

Crescent Beach

Our lives went along quietly those first months at Cross Creek. There were seldom any visitors, and it was just the two of us in the house most of the day, or three of us when Martha was there. Mrs. Rawlings would work most days, starting right after breakfast, or spend long hours reading.

But there were days when she didn't write, I couldn't say why. Sometimes after breakfast she'd say, "Idella, pack up some things, and we'll have lunch over at the beach." And that's what we'd do, no matter what the time of year. Mrs. Rawlings owned a cottage at Crescent Beach, just south of St. Augustine, and sometimes we'd drive over in the morning, have lunch, and drive back to Cross Creek the same afternoon. Other times she'd want to spend a day or two, sometimes longer, depending on her mood. I had to stay packed.

My friends in Reddick thought my job was exciting, because I got to go places with Mrs. Rawlings. It was, but it was also hard work. It got so I didn't look forward to these sudden trips, because of all the extra work it meant for me. I'd be cleaning up one place, thinking about all the work I'd have to do when we got to the other place. But I never complained, I just kept on working and doing and keeping myself to myself.

It took a little over an hour to drive to the beach cottage from Cross Creek. Nowadays with speed limits and traffic lights and so many cars on the road, it takes longer, but as I have said before, Mrs. Rawlings was not one to drive slow or take much heed of speed limits. We drove that road so often, back and forth, that we knew it well, and when you know a road well you drive it faster. Most times we would drive north on 301 to Hawthorne, then turn east onto Route 20 and follow it to Hastings. These roads were paved and easy to drive. But at Hastings we turned east onto an unpaved road, and from there on over to the beach it was twelve or so miles of the loneliest dirt road you ever saw.

Even today it's a lonely road, with very few houses on it for miles. I drove along it just recently, and thought about what might have happened to me out there all alone—a flat tire, or an accident? It would have been a long time before help arrived. But I was young then, and I never gave a thought to things like hopping into the car and making the trip to the beach, lonely roads or no lonely roads. Sometimes I'd drive over and back twice in one day, if something had been left behind at Cross Creek, and thought nothing of that either.

Wrong Turn on a Stormy Day

I remember one time when the danger of that lonely dirt road did make itself plain. We set out from Cross Creek one stormy afternoon, headed for the beach. We were in two cars, Mrs. Rawlings and Mr. Baskin, her gentleman friend, in his car, and Martha and I in Mrs. Rawlings' car. There must have been a party scheduled or some special doings, because Martha seldom came to the beach. This day I would be glad of her company.

We started out together, Mr. Baskin driving in front and me following, keeping him in sight all the way to Hastings. This was

I show some recent visitors (1990) Marjorie Kinnan Rawlings' favorite spot for writing, on the porch at Cross Creek.

not always easy, because the rain was teeming down so heavy you could hardly see. Florida rain is like that, and hard to drive in because the heavy rain makes huge puddles on the road that are frightening to drive through. So it was slow going at times, and both cars had to keep their headlights on to see through the downpour.

At Hastings, where he should have turned right onto the dirt road toward the beach, Mr. Baskin just kept right on driving north, toward St. Augustine. I didn't know what to think. No one had told me they were going into St. Augustine, but I thought, well, they have an appointment or decided to do some shopping or something, and they forgot to tell me. Naturally, if they had things to do, I wasn't supposed to come along, so I turned east onto the dirt road as usual.

Before long the road had turned to mud and the rain was coming down harder than ever, and I could go no further. I pulled over and turned the car off, and Martha and I sat there, talking and shivering in the damp, waiting for the rain to let up and help to come. It was getting dark, and we had been stuck in the mud for five long hours and no one had come by, and we began to worry that no help was coming.

Finally, here came some headlights. It was a car, driving toward us from the east, the direction of the beach. It slowed and stopped, and out hopped Mr. Baskin.

"Why didn't you follow us?" he wanted to know. "We took the paved roads up through St. Augustine and back down. We never thought you'd try to get through that dirt road in this storm."

We were so glad to see him, we didn't even mind being chastised. To myself I thought that if we had been white friends and not colored servants, they might have pulled over and told us what they were doing and why. But we were so used to white folks doing as they pleased, while we were supposed to keep on with our work, that we just assumed that this was such a case. But there was no use trying to explain that. Just let them think we were stupid.

The Beach Cottage

The dirt road ended at Route A1A, which runs along the beach, and from there it was only a few blocks to the cottage. There were very few houses on Crescent Beach in those days. I can only recall maybe nine or ten houses in the vicinity, and only one that was close by Mrs. Rawlings' house. At the junction of A1A and the dirt road from Hastings there was a store where you could buy food and gas or pick up a newspaper. You'd never guess looking at the houses and stores all crowded together now that Crescent Beach was once just a tiny little settlement.

The cottage was small and box-shaped, painted yellow with

Marjorie Kinnan Rawlings' cottage at Crescent Beach. Courtesy of the Rawlings Collection, Rare Books and Manuscripts, University of Florida Libraries.

white trim. It was set off the road, way up on top of some high, rolling dunes. It was situated in such a way that after you parked the car, you had to climb up some steep wooden Z-shaped steps to get to the house, which was much higher than the garage and the parking area. There was a landing halfway up the stairs, and a good thing too, because I always had food and bags and all kinds of things to carry up those stairs. The landing gave me a chance to set things down and rest a minute before making the rest of the climb.

The kitchen door and the back of the house were at the top of the stairs; the front of the house faced the ocean, and you couldn't see it until you went out onto the beach.

The cottage at Crescent Beach was not fancy at all, and neither was the house at Cross Creek. Many times I've heard visitors say the house at Cross Creek doesn't look like a rich woman's house, and the little beach cottage doesn't either. The present owners of the beach cottage have built rooms on and remodeled the cottage considerably, but it's still a modest little house.

Mrs. Rawlings wasn't rich when she bought those houses, but she loved them and kept them, even when she had plenty of money and could have bought something much larger and fancier. She was a plain, no-nonsense sort of woman, and her houses suited her fine.

Mrs. Rawlings was especially attached to the house at Cross Creek and didn't care if people thought it was grand or not. She just didn't care about those things. She was not pretentious at all, and although she could be *most* particular about food and the way it was served, she cared very little about having fine houses or fancy dresses.

The beach cottage had a tiny kitchen, two bedrooms, one quite large, the other much smaller, one bathroom, and a good-sized living/dining room. None of the rooms were very large, but with the picture windows looking out on the ocean they seemed big and airy.

The house was several hundred yards back from the beach, surrounded by sea oats and grasses, with a clear, spectacular view of the ocean. The furnishings were modern, and it seemed to me that this house was a real improvement over the old-fashioned house at Cross Creek.

There were palmetto bushes all around the house, and tall sea grass. At the bottom of the stairs was a long hedge of oleanders, such a pretty sight when their pink and white flowers were in bloom. At certain times of year, our handyman, Mr. Leyton, would plant petunias there, too. It was a beautiful place.

My quarters were in the garage down below, which had a tiny room attached that was my bedroom. Later Mrs. Rawlings converted the entire two-car garage into a nice little apartment for me, with everything I needed except a kitchen. I always had to climb up to the house to cook and eat.

Rattlesnakes!

The only thing that worried me some was the rattlesnakes, which were everywhere. There were so many in those bushes between the house and the road, that I had to take the car and drive the hundred or so yards to the mailbox to pick up the mail. I didn't dare walk, even that short way. Many's the time a big old diamondback rattlesnake would crawl right in front of the car, taking his time getting across the road, and I'd stop and wait until he slithered off into the bushes, because Mrs. Rawlings told me never to run over big snakes, because they could turn the car over. Foolish as it sounds, I believed her. She also told me to keep the windows up on the way to the mailbox and, as always, I did exactly what she said. Hot in that car? You can just imagine, but I did as I was told.

At night I would hear a peculiar cracking and snapping noise coming from the palmetto tree outside my bedroom window. When I asked Mr. Leyton what the noise could be, he said it was probably rattlesnakes crawling around. After that I shut my window, sea breeze or no sea breeze. There was a screen on the window, but I didn't trust it to keep snakes out.

Mrs. Rawlings had respect for snakes, but she was not as afraid of them as I was. One morning when I brought her breakfast tray to her bedroom at the cottage, she spied a little snake lying near the window.

"Run, get the broom, Idella," she whispered, and when I came back she killed the snake herself. That is some woman, I thought. I don't think I ever met a more independent and self-sufficient woman than Mrs. Rawlings when she had to be. If there had been a man around, I'm sure she'd have asked him to take care of the snake. But there wasn't, so she did what had to be done herself.

The best example of Mrs. Rawlings' respect for snakes happened at Cross Creek. Martha went into Mrs. Rawlings' bathroom one morning and found a big old snake coiled up in the toilet. She ran screaming to Mrs. Rawlings, who grabbed the quilt off her bed and stuffed it in on top of the snake. Then she got in her car and roared off to Silver Springs to get her friend Ross Allen, who was a famous authority on snakes. She planned to bring him home with her and have him capture the snake and take it away.

By the time Mrs. Rawlings got back with Mr. Allen, Martha had gone and got Little Will, and Little Will had killed the snake. Mrs. Rawlings was hopping mad. She railed on and on about the time she had wasted, and why didn't we wait till she got back, and here was Mr. Allen come all the way from Silver Springs all for nothing. Such cussing as you never heard! But I was glad the snake was gone, and from that day to this I always look in the toilet before I sit down.

I Go to School

One day, soon after World War II started, we were driving from Cross Creek over to the beach cottage. I can see Mrs. Rawlings now, plain as day, sitting in the car wearing her short fur cape and smoking her cigarette.

Suddenly she turned to me and said, "Idella, is there anything—anything at all—that you'd like to do after I'm dead?"

Well, this question took me completely by surprise, and I thought she was making a joke.

"After you're dead? Mrs. Rawlin's, you know that I am going to die long before you do. I'm going to work myself to death!"

"No, I'm serious, Idella," she persisted. "What would you like to do? I don't *ever* want you to have to work in another white woman's kitchen."

Well, for some reason, this remark of hers made me mad. I was as mad as I am black, and that is pretty mad. Here she was, saying she didn't want me to have to work for someone else, but it didn't seem to matter how hard I worked for her. All I *did* was work, hard as a dog. Clean up one house, move to another, clean that one up and turn around and go back to the first. But of course, I could never say that to her, so I just got quiet and said nothing.

A few miles later, when we were just about to the beach, I said, "Mrs. Rawlin's, there *is* something I've always wanted to do."

"Idella! What is it?"

"I have always wanted to learn to do people's hair, to be a beautician."

She thought about this for a moment, then said, "Well, do you know where there is a beauty school you can go to?" Yes, I did, and I told her: the Apex School in Atlanta.

"Well, dammit, that's good," she exclaimed. "Now I won't have to go into Ocala to have my hair done!"

Within two weeks, she had everything set up and ready for me to go to Atlanta. She took care of all of it: fees, tools, living arrangements, everything. As soon as I was registered at Apex and had all my tools, ready to start the course, the director asked me to come to his office.

"Miss Thompson," he said, "Mrs. Rawlings has made arrangements for you to work on white ladies' hair, too. These ladies cannot (what he meant was "will not") come here during the day, but they will be here after hours at night and come in through the back door, and the instructors will teach you how to work on them."

So it was arranged. I was grateful to Mrs. Rawlings for doing all this for me, of course. But don't forget that I was young and wanted to have fun, too. When the other girls were done at school, they would go off to the U.S.O. and spend the evenings dancing and flirting with the handsome young servicemen. Meanwhile, Idella was back at Apex, spending her evenings working on white ladies' hair. You can imagine there were some evenings when I felt less grateful than I should have.

The beauty course was to have lasted about nine months, but it took me a little longer, because I heard of an even better school in Tampa, where a friend of mine was enrolled. I figured Tampa would also be nearer home, and I asked to go there. Mrs. Rawlings made the arrangements again, and I finished the course at Angelo's Beauty College. All the time I was away, we kept in touch. I would write and tell her how the course was going and what I was learning, and she would write back that things were fine.

From time to time she would send me packages, little things she thought I might need. Once I mentioned my white uniform blouse was getting worn out and looked a little shabby, and she sent me a new one in the next mail.

When I got back from the beauty school, I took up my old job as if nothing had ever happened. People often ask me if I did Mrs. Rawlings' hair after I came back, but I didn't. She wanted me to, but I didn't. When I came back, things were worse than ever. Mrs. Rawlings was drinking more than ever, she wasn't getting much writing done other than letters, which made her cranky, and she was harder than ever to reason with. I had my hands full dealing with her every day, never mind do her hair.

Walking to Butler's Beach

Mrs. Rawlings would get up early when she was at the cottage and take a long walk on the beach. She always took the dog with her and walked for miles and miles. In the afternoons, when I had finished cooking and cleaning, I would walk too. Sometimes we would walk together, and these walks were one of the most enjoyable things to do at the beach. The ocean was beautiful to see, and there was almost always bright sunshine and a breeze off the water. I loved to sit on the beach and watch the boats far off or just watch the waves. To get away from the summer heat at Cross Creek and come to the beach was pure pleasure. In winter months we had cozy fireplaces and gas heaters, and that was nice too.

On my walks with the dog, Pat, I often headed north toward

St. Augustine. One day, about two years after I first started coming to the beach, I spotted some dark little figures way, way off in the distance. It looked like quite a crowd of people, so I decided to walk toward them and get a closer look. After walking more than a mile, I could see that they were black people, and my steps quickened. In all it was about two miles, but well worth the long walk, because there on the beach I met people who would soon become good friends.

Every Wednesday the shops closed at noon in St. Augustine, and many of the better class of young black workers came to this beach. It was called Butler's Beach, after the black businessman who owned it. Mr. Butler owned property in town too, and he had a tiny little nightclub there on the beach. This was the only beach where black people could go to swim and enjoy the beach, and the little nightclub was the scene of many happy evenings of talking, dancing, laughing, and making friends.

If they wondered where I had come from or why I was out on the beach all alone with a dog, they didn't say so. One handsome young man with a big smile and a more than friendly gleam in his eye was the first to greet me with "Hi, where you goin'?" We made some informal introductions, and after a nice swim, we had a long chat on the beach.

Before I headed back to the cottage, I accepted an invitation to come and visit a certain combination drugstore and ice cream parlor in St. Augustine. One of the young men I met that day was a dentist; another was the druggist who owned the drugstore and ice cream parlor. They assured me that a nice crowd of people came there regularly, and we parted with a promise that I would come into town soon.

Trouble Begins

It was lonely for me at the beach. At least at the Creek I had Martha to talk to. There were a few other black girls who worked at other beach cottages. One was a girl from Palatka, another was from Hastings. I would sometimes run into them in the little store at Crescent Beach when I went to get the newspaper, but they were only at the beach on weekends.

There was really very little for me to do at the beach when my work was done except read or write letters. I was longing for some friends and fun and company after so many years out at Cross Creek. In her book *Cross Creek*, Mrs. Rawlings wrote that one of the things she liked about her "perfect maid" was that I wasn't interested in men. I have often wondered why Mrs. Rawlings would say such a thing in her book, a book that would be read by many people, those who knew me and many more who didn't. Those who knew me knew that I had taken the job with Mrs. Rawlings in the first place because of trouble with a man in West Palm Beach.

The truth was I was plenty interested in men; there just weren't any at Cross Creek, or at least none that appealed to me. Now, at Butler's Beach, I had met several young men who were very attractive, and I guess you might say that's when the clouds started to form on the horizon as far as my relationship with Mrs. Rawlings was concerned. In fact, my interest in men, I'm afraid, was greater than hers. She already had a steady man friend in Norton Baskin, whereas I was unattached, and that's how the trouble started.

I was as good as my word. As soon as I had an afternoon free, I took Mrs. Rawlings' car and headed for the drugstore in St. Augustine. This place was everything the owner had said it was, and more. It was a nice, clean place, and all the best young black people gathered there. I made friends who invited me to their church, and from then on I was running to St. Augustine every chance I got.

I got a lot of chances, because when Mrs. Rawlings was writing at the cottage, she did not want or need me around. She would have me fix something for lunch or dinner, and tell me to take the day off.

I always drove Mrs. Rawlings' car and dressed nicely, and my new friends thought I was rich and this fine car belonged to me. I admit, I didn't tell them any different. One day a young man I knew must have seen Mrs. Rawlings driving the car, because he asked me, "Idella, didn't I see a white lady driving your car the other day?"

"Oh," I replied casually, "that's a friend of mine. I let her drive the car every once in while."

I was grateful for the car. It was my freedom, and I drove it far more than even Mrs. Rawlings thought. I drove to Jacksonville to see my sisters. Hettie was teaching nursing and Dorothy was a student nurse at Brewster Hospital. I drove to Florida Normal College, now called Florida Memorial College, in St. Augustine, where at one time or another my other two sisters and my brother, E.M., were students. I spent a lot of time on that campus. I even drove groups of my new friends to Tampa or Jacksonville to see football games. Mrs. Rawlings was so involved in her work that she never asked where I had been or what I had done, and I never told her.

Mrs. Rawlings Buys a Ticket

I got involved in helping to support Florida Normal College, not only because my sisters and brother were there, but because all the black churches in central Florida had to contribute toward the school to keep it running. The school was about four or five miles west of St. Augustine, and was supported by all the black Baptist churches. At my church in Reddick, we were forever selling pies or having fund-raisers for the school, and helping the school had been a regular part of our church work for as long as I could remember. Each church member would be given tickets to sell for ten cents apiece. There was no raffle or drawing or any type of prize for buying these tickets. They were just tickets, and when you bought one you received nothing but the satisfaction that you had helped a worthy cause.

One week I had some tickets to sell. We were at Cross Creek, and I was sitting on the green woodbox on the kitchen porch, where I often sat after my work was done. I was sitting there wondering what Mrs. Rawlings was going to say, for I had made up my mind to ask her to buy one of these ten-cent tickets. After lunch, Little Will was to drive me over to Reddick in the truck to visit Mama, and I was determined to get up my courage and ask her before I left. As she left the dining room and walked past me, I summoned my courage and asked her if she would buy one of my tickets.

"What tickets, Idella?"

I told her all about the school, and when I would have to report in with the money.

"All right," she said, "I'll have something for you before you leave."

After lunch she handed me a check for $150, made out to Florida Normal College, and for many years afterwards she helped with a generous check for the school. It was then that I began to realize how generous Mrs. Rawlings was when it came to people or organizations that really needed help.

Over the years there would be many times when I would see her reach out to help others. I can think of many a Christmas when we were away somewhere and she'd be worrying about getting back in time to bring Christmas to Cross Creek. She bought presents for everyone she knew there who was in need.

Mrs. Rawlings never minded giving money or whatever to anyone she thought really needed it. But she never cared much about buying things for herself, not like some rich folks. She seemed to take much more pleasure in giving to others and was generous and kind as she could be. If she saw my blouse was getting worn, she'd give me the car keys and some money and tell me to go to Wilson's in Gainesville and buy a new blouse, never thinking to get something new for herself. She was always thinking of other people, with little regard for herself.

Mrs. Rawlings took an interest in all the families around Cross Creek, but one family was particularly special to her: the Fountains. Martha Mickens' daughter Sissie and her husband, Henry Fountain, had seven or eight children at least, and the family was very poor. These children were often around the house, because they only lived down the road and around a bend, in a little house on the banks of Cross Creek. They would come over late in the morning and carry home a bucket of Dora's milk, or some treat we had saved for them. At Christmastime, Mrs. Rawlings bought presents for all of them, and she always seemed interested to know what they were doing.

One of the Fountain children, called Little Martha, was an especially pretty little girl, about four years old, with dark brown skin and soft straight hair. Mrs. Rawlings took a liking to the girl, and one summer day when we were packing to go to the beach cottage, she asked Sissie if Little Martha could come to the beach for a few weeks and be "her little girl." Sissie agreed, and off we went to Crescent Beach.

Now you can guess who was given charge of Little Martha for the most part, and that was Idella. I cleaned her up, so that she no longer looked dingy, and I spent hours doing her hair and putting pretty little bows in it.

Little Martha had very few clothes, so Mrs. Rawlings gave me some money and I went into St. Augustine and bought some pretty bright purple cotton cloth and made Martha a little sundress with a big hem in it. She looked as cute as she could be, all dressed up in her purple dress, with purple bows to match, and little white socks and sandals.

She was a sweet child, in the way all the time, but she gave me something to do all that summer. I spent time teaching her to speak correctly and to read and spell a little. She went with me for walks on the beach and on shopping trips, and she was a lot of company. However, she was lonesome for her playmates, and she had to spend a lot of time by herself when I was doing my work.

Little Martha was a quiet child, who liked to talk to herself and hum little songs. One afternoon I was sitting in my room reading, when I heard a soft popping noise. I looked out the door, and saw that the sound was Martha snapping her fingers to a beat only she could hear, and swaying back and forth to the rhythm. As she snapped, she was making up a little tuneless song to herself. It went like this:

Snap, snap. "I don't care what [snap] they put on me."

Snap, snap. "I don't care what [snap] they give me to eat."

Snap, snap. "I don't care where [snap] they take me."

Snap, snap. "I'm goin' back [snap] to my mama!" Snap.

That evening we went to the store for ice cream. I asked Martha if she was unhappy being at the beach, but she didn't say anything. She was only four, but she knew better than to be impolite.

Little Martha refused ever to come to the beach again. Years later I could say, "Martha, come on, let's go to the water," and she would look at me with those big brown eyes, put her foot down and say, quietly but firmly, "No."

Hettie

Mrs. Rawlings was always nice about me having visitors, especially at the beach, where she knew my sisters and brothers were nearby. Sometimes Hettie and other nurses from her hospital would take a bus and come out to the beach to visit me. Mrs. Rawlings never minded me having my sisters or their friends down at my little apartment. These visits were another reason I liked going to the cottage so much.

All my sisters and I are very close to this day, but Hettie and I have a special bond because of a shadow that crossed our lives when we were very small. In my life there have been many dark

Mama with baby Thelma in her arms (Palmetto, Florida, 1919). Left to right in front of Mama: me, age 5; E.M., age 2; and Hettie, age 6.

shadows, and the fear they caused me is maybe one of the reasons I stayed with Mrs. Rawlings so long. With Mrs. Rawlings there was safety in knowing what to expect.

The shadow between me and Hettie came about because my

Aunt Olive was childless. Olive was my Papa's sister. She and her husband, Sam, had a big house in Jacksonville and they both had good jobs. Aunt Olive was a teacher, and Uncle Sam was one of the first black men in Jacksonville to be hired as a postman. They had plenty of money, but the one thing they didn't have was a child, and they wanted one very much. And here was Papa with a house full of children and could hardly make a living for his family, for he was only sharecropping in those days.

Aunt Olive decided to help Mama and Papa by asking them to let Hettie come and live with them in Jacksonville, at least during the school year. Mama told me it was a hard decision to make, but after Aunt Olive made several trips to visit, each time begging them to let Hettie go, they agreed to send her for the next school term.

On the day she was to leave, Mama dressed Hettie up all pretty and got her ready. Hettie was given a brown paper bag with two homemade biscuits with blackberry jelly on them to eat on the train. Mama's daddy, Papa Jake, hitched his old horse, George, to the wagon. When he was ready, we climbed up over the wagon wheels, and Hettie sat on the front seat with Papa Jake. He jerked the reins and said, "Come up, George," gave George a tap with the whip, and off we went down that dusty one-lane road toward the train station at Reddick.

Soon we heard old Train Number 39 blowing her horn, and by and by it came to a stop. A man stepped off yelling, "All aboard, all aboard," and Hettie got on. This was a short train, and it moved very slowly, but it seemed to me that it left the station all too soon that day. I can see us now, sharp and clear in my mind, both of us crying and waving.

Hettie was seven and I was six when this happened, and it was the beginning of a pain that each of us still talks about. We were the closest of sisters then because we were so close in age. Thelma was five years younger, just a baby when this happened. Dorothy and Liza were about a year and a half apart in age and were as close to each other as Hettie and I were.

Hettie was my best friend, my constant companion and play-mate, and we loved each other very much. This separation was more than I could bear, and I cried and cried for weeks after she was gone, and ever after there was a sadness in me that nothing could change.

Years after we were grown, Hettie said she had never been more frightened than she was that day. She shook with fear every time the conductor came toward her asking for tickets. She had no ticket, and no idea that Uncle Sam had arranged about her ticket with the conductor. As the train slowed for Jacksonville, she still had the brown paper bag clenched in her hand; she had been too frightened to eat the biscuits on the train.

When the conductor put her off, he pointed to a strange man and woman standing on the platform, waiting. I don't suppose either of us had seen Aunt Olive or Uncle Sam more than two or three times our whole lives, but here they were, telling her what a big girl she was for making the trip all by herself.

Hettie was up there in Jacksonville, afraid, and I was back home in Reddick, lonesome and crying, feeling so alone. After that, Hettie only came home for short visits in the summer. Believe this or not, that separation was a time in our lives we never forgot. We often talk about what it did to us, and how the fear of separation haunted our lives. Even now, we feel the loss of those years we should have been together. Mama must have sensed this and felt badly about it too, for so many times after we were all grown she would say, "I don't care how many children you have, just don't separate them; keep them all together."

There were some blessings in all this for Hettie, of course. She grew up to be a refined, beautiful city girl. I remained a rough, hard-working country girl. Our lives were so different because of this separation.

Hettie could come for short visits to the beach cottage while she was teaching at the hospital, and those visits were something I looked forward to each time. Mrs. Rawlings did not know any-thing about this story in my life. All she was interested in was

Dorothy (background), Hettie (center), and Mama (right) at Hettie's house in Jacksonville, Florida (c. 1945).

My sister, Hettie L. Mills (c. 1983).

whether I could cook and keep her house, hold quiet, and let her do her work. But she must have sensed something, because every time my well-educated, professional sisters were around, she praised my work to the skies. It was as if we were both trying to convince my family that I had made a good choice of career, when everyone could see this wasn't true.

Waiting for Mr. Baskin

Mrs. Rawlings and Mr. Baskin had several friends who lived in St. Augustine. Occasionally these friends would come for dinner. There was a dropleaf table in the dining room which could seat eight people when it was fully extended, and took up almost no room at all when it was folded down. Guests would be treated to the same carefully planned meals as we might serve at Cross Creek, and afterward there might be a game of bridge. Both Mrs. Rawlings and Mr. Baskin enjoyed playing bridge, as did their friends Senator and Mrs. Verle Pope, who were frequent bridge partners.

Mr. Baskin was always working, and it seemed to me that Mrs. Rawlings was always waiting for him. When they were apart, she would write to him every day. He would try to write, too, but sometimes he would miss a day or two. The disappointment on her face, when the mail came and there was no letter from him, was sad to see.

She was always inviting him to come for weekends, and sometimes he would come, sometimes not. Many times we went over to the beach cottage, and she would make all sorts of plans to enjoy the weekend with Mr. Baskin. She'd tell me to take the car and go visit my friends in St. Augustine, which of course I did, gladly. I would spend the day, maybe run over to a ball game in Jacksonville or go to a movie, and come back that evening, only to hear her story of how Mr. Baskin couldn't make it over that weekend. As soon as I saw her, I'd know what had happened. I could read her expressions and moods like a book. Right away I'd see that she was miserable and I'd ask, "What's wrong, Mrs. Rawlin's, what is it?"

Sometimes she'd hug me and cry and tell me all about it, sometimes she'd tell me, "Go on, I'm all right." And always on these occasions, the whiskey bottle would end up being her weekend companion, and she would try to drown her disappointment.

When Mr. Baskin was around, she would glow with happiness. He was a very handsome man, with wavy blonde hair, and always impeccably dressed. He was known for his ability to tell stories and make people laugh, and whenever he was at a party, he was the center of attention. He had a remarkable, distinctive voice, and people just hung on everything he said.

When I first met him, he was manager of the Marion Hotel in Ocala. He was the perfect hotel man; he loved to be with people and to have a crowd of people around. He had charm, oh my, he had charm, and Mrs. Rawlings adored him.

Although they were very different in many ways, they had a lot in common. They both liked the beach, and liked to sit together for long hours and read silently. They swam and played bridge with friends, went to movies and to football games together.

Mr. Baskin had a sporty convertible, and they would put the top down and ride along with the wind blowing their hair, looking so happy together. She loved his attention, loved to listen to his stories and laugh with him, and was miserable when he would let her down. She would make excuses for him, saying that he had this or that to do, or he had something come up at the last minute, but I could plainly see that she was hurt when he failed to come when she wanted him to.

He tried his best to make her happy, but real happiness always seemed to be just out of her reach. To me she seemed restless, always moving from one thing to another, traveling from one place to another, always thinking that the next thing or place would make her happier.

In her mind, marriage was what would make her happy, and that was very much on my mind, too. What neither of us realized was that marriage would upset our way of life much more than either of us ever dreamed.

" F O U R "

Cross Creek Cookery

Over the years there were many visitors at Cross Creek, many of them rich and famous. People think we had company out there all the time, but in between visitors there were long stretches of time, sometimes months, when we only saw other people when we went out shopping.

When we were the only people in the house, Mrs. Rawlings would bounce into the kitchen at any time to talk. I say bounce because she walked with a heavy, bouncing step, and you could hear her coming, thump, thump, thump, loud and clear across those wood floors. She'd come to talk about cooking mostly. She enjoyed cooking! Sometimes she'd bounce in and announce that she was going to cook some dish or other.

"Idella," she'd say, "I'm going to make the biscuits tonight. You can make yours tomorrow night."

She'd stop writing some days and get up from wherever she was sitting, and maybe her mind would say, *Oh, I'll stop for today, let's go in here with Idella.* And here she'd come with "Idella, let's make this," or "What about this? Get that recipe book, let's make that." She would chat about all kinds of things: the weather, the dogs, the birds and animals around the place, or the flowers, and

Me in the kitchen at Cross Creek (1990). Photo by Carl Laundrie.

ask me what I thought about this or that. These were the happiest days between us, together in the kitchen at Cross Creek.

When she got the idea to write the cookbook, *Cross Creek Cookery*, we were months and months together in that tiny kitchen, because she was determined that every recipe would have just the right ingredients, in just the right amounts.

As I have said before, my recipes were in my hands and head. I never wrote them down until Mrs. Rawlings started on that cookbook. When I cooked, I put in a pinch of this and a pinch of that, but I couldn't say just how much of anything I used. I tasted and added like all good cooks, but she would have none of that.

I can't tell you how many times we cooked some dishes, or how much food we wasted and threw away. When something didn't come out just right, we'd cook it again and again until it did. And talk about hot! You don't know what hot is until you've fired up a wood stove on a 100-degree Florida August day! It was something, but we both loved to cook, so it was enjoyable.

Many of the recipes in the book were mine, but she only gave me credit for three of them, including "Idella's Biscuits." There were several others that were mine, too, such as the chocolate pie, and of course it was me who did most of the cooking when we were trying all the recipes out.

All I ever got from the cookbook was an autographed copy, but in those days I was grateful for any little crumb that white people let fall, so I kept my thoughts about the cookbook strictly to myself.

Dinners at the Creek

Mrs. Rawlings liked to eat, and as the years went by she had to battle with her weight. She was about five feet seven and weighed about 180 pounds and was heavy from the waist down. I'd look at those tiny little size three or four shoes sometimes and wonder how those poor little feet could carry all that weight.

She ate very little breakfast, and a light lunch, but she had a complete dinner prepared and served to her every night. You'd think we were preparing for company. I had to prepare fresh vegetables, lavish cuts of meat complete with rich sauces and gravies, fancy desserts, and cook and serve it all just as if there was a house full of company.

In the garden at Cross Creek Little Will planted okra, parsley, beans, onions, carrots, mustard and collard greens, beets, broccoli, any vegetable you could think of. Just about every vegetable we cooked came from the garden.

There was always a ham in the icebox, sunrise to sunset, and this was served in many ways. Toward the end of the ham I would grind the last meat for ham croquettes, and serve them with tiny okra and rich Hollandaise sauce, made with Dora's butter.

We were always baking. Almost every day the smell of homemade rolls, loaves of bread, pies, and many kinds of cakes filled the house. Pecan pie and fresh coconut pie were her favorites, and fresh mango ice cream. I can see myself now, peeling, mashing, and straining mangoes, mixing the cream and sugar and cranking that old ice cream maker.

She liked lamb chops and leg of lamb. We didn't do much with chicken, but sometimes had turkey. We'd drive for miles to get blue crabs or oysters, and we often served fish, either broiled, or stuffed and baked. She loved to use sherry or rum to flavor dishes, and these were always on the grocery list.

When we got crabs, we got plenty, and I would cook, clean, and pick them all and put them in the ice box to use in salads and Newburgs. If you have ever boiled crabs you know how they are, and you can imagine me in the kitchen at Cross Creek, with crabs jumping out of the big pot and crawling all over the floor. Me with a big prong catching them and putting them back in that boiling water. When finally the battle was over, the poor crabs had to give up.

Mrs. Rawlings and I shared a love for making a plate of food look beautiful. We planned meals so that colors balanced and looked good together. These things were important to both of us, and we spent many an hour discussing how this vegetable would look and taste with that meat.

Beginning in about 1947 we began to travel to Van Hornesville, New York, every summer, where Mrs. Rawlings was gathering material for a book. Even up there we had a garden, but no Little Will to tend it. Her friend, Mrs. Young, would loan us her gardener, and I had to help him.

It was much easier to grow things up there, for the soil was much richer. I especially remember the asparagus. Sand behind each eye, and *so* much trouble to wash. I was really upset whenever Mrs. Rawlings would say, "Idella, let's have asparagus tonight," because it was hard work. To this day I cringe whenever asparagus is mentioned.

Plucking Ducks

Mrs. Rawlings liked to go duck hunting. Oh yes, she could shoot. She used to stand on the back porch at Cross Creek blowing her duck call, telling me how you would call the ducks, and when they flew up, you would mow them down. Well, the first time I remember a duck hunt, she brought home three or four ducks.

She took them out of her bag, saying "Idella, pick these and we'll have them for dinner." Now believe this or not, it took me three hours to pick one duck. Mrs. Rawlings had no idea that I had never picked a duck before. Hours later, she came out on the porch to see if I had finished and saw I only had one duck half done.

As usual she yelled for Martha, who came and in no time at all had all those ducks ready to cook. But by this time it was too late to stuff and roast them for dinner. The ducks had to wait till the next day, and we had to have sandwiches and milk for dinner. Mrs. Rawlings was outdone.

"Idella, I thought all you people knew how to pick ducks and chickens."

Ducks have all those tiny pin feathers, you see, and they are hard to pull. After Martha pulled all the big feathers, she lit a piece of newspaper and singed the pin feathers, then washed the

At a party in the living room at Cross Creek (c. 1940), clockwise: state Senator Verle Pope from St. Augustine (right, standing against the back curtain); his wife, writer Edith Pope (seated); Cecil Clark (seated); Norton Baskin (standing); Marjorie Kinnan Rawlings (seated, with her back to the camera); Rebecca Camp (standing); me and my friend Elmer Shell, who came from Hawthorne to help serve dinner.

little fellow all over and they came right out. Thank you, Miss Martha, for that was one of the days I shall never forget.

Lonely, Even in a Crowd

I was at Cross Creek a long time before we ever had any visitors. The company started to arrive after *The Yearling* came out. Then all of a sudden she'd say we were going to have four, six, twelve, fourteen, or however many people for dinner. By this time she had confidence enough in me to know that all she had to do was tell me how many, and I would suggest some dishes, she would add others, and once the menu was set she could just leave everything to me. She liked to cook, and I liked to cook; liking the same thing, it was easy.

When company was coming she would get all excited and set everything aside to get ready. She loved having company; she loved to entertain. Mrs. Rawlings took great pains planning dinner parties and getting just the right foods and wines. When company came, she never let a dish go to the table unless it was one we had served many times and knew was foolproof.

But it seemed to me like she had a short time span as far as company was concerned. She liked to invite people, and she enjoyed the company, laughing and talking with her guests for a time. But she seemed to tire of it early, and acted relieved when it was over and they went home.

There were many times when she left her own party early. She'd say goodnight, or sometimes just leave the room without saying anything. It was as if she liked to plan and think about having parties more than she enjoyed the actual parties. Maybe the real thing was not as exciting as thinking about it or imagining it.

For all the company she had, she was a lonesome, lonely woman. She had few friends, and she had many visitors. She wrote to many people, and they wrote back. I don't think there was anything in this world Mrs. Rawlings enjoyed doing more than writing. If not a book, she was answering mail from friends or fans. Especially during the war, when she wrote to dozens of soldiers, the morning mail was always full of letters, and she would sit right down and answer every one of them.

She was always busy, either writing or traveling somewhere, always restless and nervous. She seemed to move from one thing to another, like she thought she'd be happy doing something new, but when she went to the new thing, it didn't make her happy after all, so she'd try another.

She was often sad, sometimes to the point where she couldn't get out of bed in the morning. I think a doctor today would say that she was subject to depression. She seldom smiled, except when we were cooking, or when someone complimented the food. That would always get a big grin from her. You hardly ever see a photograph of her smiling.

I always felt like she was looking for complete happiness and never found it, as if what she imagined and what was real were never the same thing for her. I thought sometimes it had to do with her not having any family nearby. I could go home to Reddick on Sundays, and sometimes for an hour or two during the week, when she would drop me off to see Mama. But Mrs. Rawlings didn't have any family to visit with and lean on. She really had no one on the place but the people who worked for her.

She would talk to me as we cooked together or on walks down the road at Cross Creek. She talked about her father, and how much she missed him. She talked about how she always wanted to be a boy, which maybe explains why she liked the woods and rough places so much. She talked about her brother, Arthur, so far away in Canada that I only saw him two or three times the whole time I knew Mrs. Rawlings, and then only for short visits. Mr. Baskin was too busy most of the time to see what was happening, that she was lonely and sad. He was off managing hotels, and later went off to the service, and I don't think he saw how serious the problem really was.

Whiskey, the Constant Companion

It was some time before I noticed that Mrs. Rawlings was drinking more than was good for her. And even if I did notice and wish she wouldn't drink, it was not my place to say anything. Who could I tell that would believe me?

On days when she felt like writing, she would go out and gather some flowers from the garden, put them in a vase, and set them in front of the typewriter on the round porch table. A big glass ashtray was cleaned and placed next to her, for she was what I would call a chain smoker, lighting one Lucky Strike from the other. She kept long matches in a big matchbox beside the ashtray. She would gather her pens and pencils, and her pads of yellow paper. When it started, I can't say exactly, but I began to notice that she was also placing a bottle of whiskey, wrapped in a paper bag, right alongside the typewriter.

Of course, while she was working I stayed out of her way so she could have quiet and write, so I had no idea how much she drank from that bottle each day. Many days I could tell when I brought lunch that she was about as full as she wanted to be, and most days after lunch she would lie down to sleep on the day bed on the porch.

Mrs. Rawlings Comes to Church

One Sunday evening I finished up the dinner dishes and straightened everything up, ready for Monday's meals, washed my hands and took off my apron. I was planning to take Mrs. Rawlings' car and drive to church in Reddick, as I often did on Sunday evenings. I went in to say good-night and tell her I was leaving, and just to be polite I asked if she'd like to go to church with me.

I had seen Mrs. Rawlings read the Bible from time to time, but she was not a church-goer, so I was truly amazed when she hopped right up out of her chair and said, "Why, yes, Idella, let's go!"

I have to admit that I regretted asking her immediately, because she had had far too much to drink.

I said, "Mrs. Rawlin's, don't you want to change your clothes?", hinting that she was not dressed exactly right for church. But she said no, she was fine, and off she went in her yellow culotte dress, ribbed socks that didn't match, and a pair of black T-strap shoes.

We got into the car, and thankfully she let me drive. All during the ride my mind was racing. I didn't want to take her to my church. Mama and the rest of my family and friends would be there, and I couldn't let them see Mrs. Rawlings when she was not at her best. So I was thinking, *What to do?*

The only thing I could think of was to take her to another

church, so that's what I did. We went to the Sanctified Church on the outskirts of Reddick. The church I'm talking about is not there any longer, and it was not much more than a small shack even then. It was very plain, almost bare inside. They didn't have pews, only planks balanced on stones.

Mrs. Rawlings was the only white person there. She beamed at the people around her as we took our seats, but few smiled back. They looked at me with suspicion in their eyes, as if to ask why on earth I had a white lady with me. They knew me, and they knew I was in the wrong church. Mrs. Rawlings was oblivious to the cool reception we were both getting.

There was scripture reading and singing and some mighty preaching that night, and soon the congregation forgot their visitors and got into the spirit of the service. They started clapping and stomping and dancing and shouting. The room got hotter and hotter, and the singing and praising got louder and louder. I looked over at Mrs. Rawlings, and there she was, just patting her hands together, swaying to the music, and smiling away at everyone around her. She was having herself a time!

As the service heated up, drums began to pound and people were shouting and singing, and I guess the whiskey told her to shout and sing, too, and she did.

When the plate was passed, she dropped in a generous offering, and a few people around us started nodding at her a little, in approval. The spirit was strong in that little church that night, and Mrs. Rawlings was smiling and tapping her feet to the music all the way home.

After the evening at the Sanctified Church, I was always more careful about polite invitations.

The First of Too Many Accidents

When she had too much to drink, Mrs. Rawlings sometimes got it into her head that she wanted to drive somewhere. Then we would have a fuss over the car keys. Sometimes I was able to win the argument, and I drove.

But one day she promised to let me have the car and go to see Mama, and then forgot her promise. When I reminded her that this was the day she said I could go to Reddick, she got mad at me and started cussing and storming about how I always had to be going to Reddick and so on. I could tell it was whiskey talking, because she never minded taking me to Reddick when she was herself. She grabbed the keys and stomped out to the car, shouting for me and Pat to come on.

As we careened along the sandy road toward Island Grove, we overtook a black convertible with a white canvas top. It had New York tags and four black people in it. We passed them in a cloud of dust. She was driving too fast, swerving all over because of the whiskey in her, and going on at me about why did I have to be going to Reddick all the time, and when was I coming back, and how I'd better by God get a ride back to Cross Creek because she wasn't coming for me.

We were just going into a long curve in the road when suddenly the car flipped into the air, and in one awful moment rolled over on its side facing back toward Cross Creek. All I remember was Pat, jumping over me and out the open window.

Mrs. Rawlings' head lolled back, and she appeared to be knocked out. I struggled to get up, but I could tell from the pain that I was hurt bad.

The black convertible we just passed drove up and stopped, and the people in it got out and rushed to help us. I could hear one of the men saying, "But this car just passed us," like he couldn't understand why our car was now facing back the way it came. They pulled us out of the car, shook Mrs. Rawlings till she came to, and drove us in their car back to the house at Cross Creek. Pat was already home.

Little Will and Martha came running and helped us onto the porch. Mrs. Rawlings said she was all right, but she wasn't all right. I was hurt worse than she was, though, so she told Little Will to get the truck and take me to the doctor in McIntosh. Dr. Strange knew Mrs. Rawlings. He patched up my broken ribs and said I was lucky my back wasn't broken. I could have been paralyzed for life, he said.

"You stay with that woman long enough," he warned me, "and she'll kill you."

After I had seen the doctor, Little Will drove me home to Reddick. News of the wreck had already reached my family, I don't know how, and Papa was on his way in his truck. We met him on the road, and he turned around and followed us home. Mama was furious with Mrs. Rawlings. She kept reminding me that she had told me so, that woman was no good.

A few days later Mrs. Rawlings came to my house to see how I was doing. Mama wouldn't let her in. She stood in the door and told her not to come in. But Mrs. Rawlings brushed right by Mama and came in anyway.

Several days later she came again, and again refused to listen to Mama when she told her not to come in. This time she came in and sniffed the air.

"What's that wonderful smell?"

It was white beans with ham and rice Mama was cooking. Mrs. Rawlings bounced right into the kitchen, got herself a bowlful, and sat right down and ate some. Mama was about fit to be tied, but Mrs. Rawlings didn't seem to notice. Mama hated her more than ever after that. She fussed about Mrs. Rawlings all during the weeks I was home recuperating.

We Go to the Movies

One afternoon a few too many cocktails got us into an adventure that still frightens me, and that was our trip to the movies. Mrs. Rawlings bounced into the kitchen right after lunch and said, "Idella, get on your dress, we're going to Ocala to the movies."

She knew I wouldn't go anywhere in my maid's uniform; that's why she told me to put on a dress. But when she said "we" were going to the movies, I knew we were headed for trouble.

The movie theater in Ocala was a "whites only" movie theater during the day. Blacks were allowed in for the evening show only, and they would have to sit in the balcony, well away from the white people. She knew that. But, "Hurry up," she said, and I did what she told me, as usual.

She let me drive, thank God, and we went into Ocala. When we got there, she said, "Put me out, and you park and come on in."

Before I could say, "Mrs. Rawlin's, I can't go in there," she was gone.

I parked the car, and walked up to the man in the ticket window. I could see another man standing outside the theater door, dressed up like a doorman. I didn't have to say a thing, the man in the ticket booth spoke to me.

"Where you goin', nigger?"

"I want a ticket to go in."

By this time still another man had appeared. The man in the ticket window sat there glaring at me, and the two others crowded in around me.

"You know you can't go in there, you go in after six o'clock."

I knew that, and Mrs. Rawlings knew it too, but she was already inside the theater. I was trying to think what to do.

"Well, will you please just take these car keys to Mrs. Rawlin's, and tell her I'm going over to my cousin's house, and I'll walk back to pick her up?" My cousin, Reverend C.P. "Pink" Brown, was pastor of the Mount Moriah Baptist Church, and lived in the church parsonage not too many blocks away. I could go there and wait for her.

They wouldn't take the keys, but one of the men went in, and in less than a minute here she came, walking fast, and those heels just thumping on the marble floor of the theater. She grabbed me and pushed me along in front of her, storming mad, just cussing at those two men.

"You get in here, Idella. What are you doing standing out here? You come in here with me. Get on in there." Like she was the boss of the theater.

She let those men have an earful of some strong language. My, that woman could cuss. They were struck dumb. They stood there with their mouths hanging open, and in we went.

She led me to a seat and sat down next to me, and we watched the movie. To this day I couldn't tell you what movie we saw, or who was in it. I sat very still, frightened to death. I thought sure that any minute a policeman would appear and yank us out of there and arrest us both, or at least arrest me. But nothing happened. We watched the movie and went on home to Cross Creek.

I have always thought that if she had not been Marjorie Kinnan Rawlings, we would never have gotten away with it. But local people became very accommodating and polite when her name was mentioned. When I went to stores and told people that Mrs. Rawlings sent me for this or that, I always got the best of service, even in Island Grove. She was famous, and at least in our area people treated her different. This made my life easier on many occasions, and on that day I was real glad she was who she was.

Feeling Left Out

I didn't drink, and sometimes I was made fun of for it. There would be a dinner party at Cross Creek, and all the guests would have cocktails. Pretty soon, Martha and the other Mickens family members would be invited in and given some drinks too. Then the guests would get them to sing.

The Mickenses laughed at me.

"Idella don't drink. She'll get a glass of water."

This whole mess made me mad, partly because of the drink-

After dinner, in the living room at Cross Creek (c. 1940), clockwise: state Senator Verle Pope from St. Augustine (seated, far right); Marjorie Kinnan Rawlings (sitting on floor); Norton Baskin (sitting on floor); Cecil Clark (seated in chair); Sissy Fountain (standing); Alberta, Little Will Mickens' girlfriend; Henry Fountain; Martha Mickens; and Little Will Mickens. Courtesy of the Rawlings Collection, Rare Books and Manuscripts, University of Florida Libraries.

ing, but mostly because of the way Mrs. Rawlings and her guests made fun of us black people right to our faces, and supposed that we were too stupid to know it. I would leave the room and just sit on that old green bench on the back porch, looking mad. Dinner would have to be rewarmed, and it would be long hours before I could clean up and get to bed, all because of whiskey.

I felt sorry for her; I still do. But there were times when I couldn't take her any more. It's hard to explain what she was like to work for, so I'll just say that every so often her problems got to be just too much for me. The first time this happened was right after *Cross Creek Cookery* came out.

I kept in touch with a cousin of mine from Reddick, named Luverne. She was working out on Long Island for some rich white people, and every time she wrote home we heard about the big money she was making. I was making a good wage myself; Mrs. Rawlings had raised my pay to five dollars a week not long after I came to Cross Creek, and that was more than almost anyone I knew made, but Luverne made four times that much.

When the troubles with Mrs. Rawlings got to be more than I could bear, I contacted Luverne, who got me a job right away with a Jewish family called Richards in Hewlett, Long Island. Not that I ever had trouble finding work, but this time I was doubly confident, for I had my autographed copy of *Cross Creek Cookery* to show who I was. I was sorry to leave Mrs. Rawlings, but I just had to get away, so off I went to New York.

The Richards family wasted no time letting others know that they had a girl from Florida who had worked for the author of *The Yearling,* and they paid me a lot more than Mrs. Rawlings did. As often as possible I used the menus from Cross Creek, even though they weren't used to too many Florida dishes.

One day I was asked to fix broiled liver for lunch, and I was told not to get it too well done, only medium rare. Now at Cross Creek we only had a wood stove, and it had no broiler. I had never fixed liver before, and never used a broiler, either. But I put the liver in a pan and put it under the broiler, and cooked it for what seemed to me long enough and took it to the table. Oh, how that lady got on me!

"This liver is raw," she fumed. "What kind of food did you fix at that Cross Creek place?"

I didn't answer her, for let's not forget that this was years before civil rights, and I was a long way from home. Humble and quiet was my way of life.

One morning Mrs. Richards asked me to help her think of something to fix for a fancy luncheon that she was to attend at the Waldorf Astoria. I told her I thought ham would be nice, and told her all the things she should buy so I could fix it.

She went to the market and got everything, and brought home a large pink salmon, too. The fish was as large as the ham, and I was amazed, for we only had salmon in cans at home. I baked the salmon and couldn't resist nibbling the delicious crusty edges of it when it was done.

Well, I fixed that ham the Cross Creek way. First it was boiled in water, wine, and brown sugar. Then I removed the skin and scored the fat in tiny squares and pushed a clove into each square. Then the ham was baked at about 125 degrees in the oven, and glazed with honey, brown sugar, and wine. I put it on a beautiful heavy sliver platter and garnished it with pineapple and cherries, and put parsley all around the edges. It was a lovely sight to see, and without even tasting it I knew it was good.

That evening Mrs. Richards told me that all the ladies raved about the ham and wanted the recipe. I replied that she should tell the ladies I didn't have a recipe, but I would fix one for them any time.

Lost and Found in Harlem

I was staying in Harlem, only a few blocks from the famous Apollo Theater, and taking the train out to Long Island every day to work for Mrs. Richards. On afternoons off and on weekends, I loved to go to the live shows.

One afternoon, I came out of the theater and found that it had gotten dark while I was in the show, and I had come out a side door. I hadn't been in New York very long, and all the buildings looked alike to me. For the life of me, I couldn't remember which way my apartment was.

Finally, I decided to hail a taxi. I'll never forget the disgusted look on that driver's face when I gave him the address. "You don't need a cab, lady," he growled at me. "That's only around the corner." I felt like a real country girl.

I hadn't been in New York long when I got a letter from Mrs. Rawlings. To this day I wonder how she got my address. I know Mama didn't give it to her, and I still can't imagine who did! She wrote that she was in the Columbia-Presbyterian Hospital in New York, and would be there a few more days and wanted me to call her.

I did as I was told, as always, but I waited three days to do it, kind of hoping that she would not be there. But the voice on the telephone was unmistakable.

"Idella, when are you coming to see me?"

I went, and we came to an agreement, and before I knew it I was back at Cross Creek working for her again. She said she needed me, and I was homesick for Mama, so back I came.

Soon after I returned, I was telling Mrs. Rawlings about my job out on Long Island, and all about how the ladies loved the ham, when she suddenly interrupted me.

"Idella, that's strange. I was just in New York, at that same hotel, and I was asked what kind of food we eat here at Cross Creek."

Well, surely you must know that I told about this experience at the wrong time of day—that is, when too much whiskey had been taken—because she got it in her mind that we would show those New York people a thing or two and ship them a Cross Creek ham.

Sure enough, she went out and bought one.

"Idella, I want you to fix this ham."

Just imagine now, from Ocala to New York this ham had to be shipped by train. I don't even know who she sent it to. I don't think it could have been in very good shape by the time it got there, but she sent it anyway.

"Now we'll let them know what kind of food we people eat down here," she said.

Everyone thought that was so clever, and she seemed to get a kick out of sending that ham to show some New Yorker that we knew how to cook and eat in Florida. When she made up her mind about something, she was determined to see it through until the thing came out her way.

In the fall of 1990 I saw a television interview with Kitty Dukakis, whose book *Now You Know* had just been published. She told about her addiction to alcohol, the depressions she had. When her family took away her alcohol, Mrs. Dukakis would drink anything with the name alcohol on it, even fingernail polish remover.

How this made me think of my friend, Mrs. Rawlings! The difference between these two women was that Mrs. Dukakis had family to see that she got help. I was sorry for Mrs. Rawlings, and my love for her grew because it seemed she had only me and her dogs to depend on. This is maybe one of the reasons I kept leaving and coming back, for she did depend on me.

She told me many things I am sure she would never have told anyone else, and she leaned on me in ways that few people ever knew. She was a good, kind woman who never meant anybody harm. The person she hurt most was herself. So our relationship was a close one, but it was one that often felt burdensome to me. Still, I did my best to protect her and help her as much as I could. I loved her then, and I love her still. What else could I do?

A Note from Mrs. Roosevelt

When Mrs. Rawlings was invited to the White House, I drove her to Ocala to catch the train. I wanted to send Mrs. Roosevelt some fresh flowers from Florida, so I polished up a beautiful silver bowl, and I cut fresh magnolia blossoms and put them in the bowl with water and moss, and packed the bowl in ice.

The next week I had a note from Eleanor Roosevelt herself, thanking me for the flowers. She said that they were lovely, although they had not lasted the trip very well, but she wanted to thank me for the idea of sending them. She said that she would be coming to Florida and looked forward to meeting me. Imagine, how nice she was to take the time to write to me.

Mrs. Rawlings invited Mrs. Roosevelt to stay at the beach cottage, and I was to be there to cook for her, but at the last minute the plans were changed. Mrs. Roosevelt never came to the cottage, nor to Cross Creek, and I was sorry that I never got to meet her. I would have been honored to meet and cook for a First Lady gracious enough to thank a servant for a bowl of wilted flowers!

Visits from Zora

Not long ago there was a Zora Neale Hurston festival in Orlando. Celebrities came to honor the black author from Eatonville with readings, talks, seminars, dinners, and such. The publicity surrounding this event got me to thinking about the two times I met Zora. The first was about 1940. How Mrs. Rawlings met Zora I don't really know, although I suspect that they might have been introduced at Rollins College in Orlando, where they both went from time to time to speak to groups of students and so on.

What I do know is that Mrs. Rawlings came running into the kitchen at Cross Creek one morning with a letter, all excited that someone named Zora would be coming to visit, and could we plan something nice for lunch. Mrs. Rawlings said that Zora Hurston was a writer, but I could not say I had heard of her before.

When the day arrived, and Zora drove up to the house, I was struck dumb. The woman was black! And here was Mrs. Rawlings, inviting her in and sitting her down on the porch like she was the queen of England. Zora was dressed plainly, not in the turban and robes she later affected. She was tall and thin and brown-skinned, and she held herself in a very proud, imperious way. The two women sat out on the porch and began to talk, and I went to my work in the kitchen. I could hear them begin to loosen up and laugh and talk a little louder, and I guessed that Mrs. Rawlings was pouring drinks for them both. I served lunch to them, but they hardly noticed me, they just kept right on talking. As the afternoon wore on, the chatter and laughter began to get louder and louder, and it was obvious that both women had had quite a lot of whiskey. Soon it began to get dark, and when I went in to see if Zora was staying for dinner, it was plain that Zora was in no shape to be driving home that day. Zora would spend the night, Mrs. Rawlings said, and she could sleep with me in the tenant house.

Imagine this now! Here was a black author who had come to visit Mrs. Rawlings and had been treated like an equal all day long, talking, laughing, and drinking together on the porch for all the world to see. But when it came to spending the night, Zora would be sent out to sleep with the servants. This was not for lack of bedrooms, mind you. Mrs. Rawlings had two empty bedrooms in the house, and no one else staying in either one.

Zora came down the path to the tenant house and slept with me in my double bed. Not much was said between us that night. We were both tired, and Zora had been drinking all day. She asked me which side of the bed I wanted her to sleep on, and I showed her where to wash up and use the outhouse, and that was the extent of our conversation. In the morning it was chilly, so I loaned Zora a small handmade quilt that Mama had made for me, and Zora put the quilt around her shoulders to keep warm. I never will forget that visit, because Zora carried that quilt with her when she left, and I never did get it back.

Years later, after Mrs. Rawlings had married and was living at Castle Warden in St. Augustine, she received another letter saying that Zora Hurston was coming to visit. She was returning from a trip to Bimini, and we were all excited that Zora was coming back from overseas. Again, there was a flurry of special preparations, and Mrs. Rawlings was excited to see her old friend again.

This time when Zora arrived, she came up to the penthouse by the back stairs. She looked poor and tired and broken. It looked like Zora has fallen on some hard times. She didn't stay long, and Mrs. Rawlings was saddened by this visit.

Later I heard that Zora was working as a waitress in a diner in Apopka to keep body and soul together, and I shook my head to think that someone with so much talent had fallen so low.

The word among the black community was that back in Eatonville Zora had acted so uppity and superior to her own people that they had rejected and shunned her. She had no friends among her own race, and white people had let her down when she had troubles.

I was not surprised to hear, years later, that Zora had died penniless and had been buried in an unmarked grave. I think the grave was unmarked on purpose. After all, there is no shame in dying poor; black people die poor every day, but their graves are still marked. Zora's grave was unmarked because her educated airs, her colorful life-style, and the way she treated her own people caused them hurt and resentment.

My mind keeps going back to the way Mrs. Rawlings made her sleep out in the tenant house. No matter how much she respected Zora's writing ability and enjoyed her company, Zora was still colored, and would always be treated as such by white people. As liberal and understanding as Mrs. Rawlings was about the poor treatment of blacks by whites, she couldn't bring herself to let a black woman sleep in her house.

In Sickness and in Health

In spite of the bad times, life in general went on happily for several years, going back and forth from Cross Creek to the cottage at Crescent Beach. In 1940 and 1941 there were many beautiful

My first husband, Bernard Young (c. 1944).

days for both of us. Mrs. Rawlings was always planning dinners, having company, and eagerly waiting for Mr. Baskin, who she seemed to love with her whole heart. I had met Bernard.

Bernard Young was a barber, one of the many people I met at that ice cream parlor in St. Augustine. He was a handsome man, tall and slim, with lovely wavy hair and beautiful white teeth. He dressed well, always stylish and neat, and I was crazy about him. Bernard was divorced and had two small children, Charlie and Beezie.

It wasn't long after we met that Bernard and I had a good relationship going. We had many friends in St. Augustine, and we would meet at one of their homes to play cards or enjoy some type of entertainment. They were all nice people, church-going types, and this certainly met with my approval, for I had been brought up in a strong Christian family and always went to church wherever we went.

One night Mrs. Rawlings and I went into St. Augustine. I drove, and put Mrs. Rawlings off at a friend's house where she was going to a party. We agreed that when she was ready to leave she would call Bernard's mother's house and I would come pick her up.

My friends and I were having a lovely evening when suddenly, about nine o'clock, I became very sick. Bernard's mother called Mrs. Rawlings at the party, and Mrs. Rawlings told Mrs. Young that I had better be taken to the hospital. She would meet us there, and she wanted Bernard to bring her car so she could have it to drive home in. I didn't really think that it was necessary to go to a hospital, but as always I did what I was told to do.

I had to have my appendix out, and I must have been sicker than I thought, because I ended up staying in Flagler Hospital for six long weeks. Mrs. Rawlings paid for all of it. She saw to it that I had a nurse in my room all day long. This nurse read, wrote, crocheted, and kept me company all that time. I had nothing but the best of care.

Since this was the early forties, blacks and whites were not in the same part of the hospital. At this hospital there was a long walkway leading from the white part of the hospital to the black side.

I had no trouble knowing when Mrs. Rawlings was coming down that long walk, she walked so hard, sometimes stumbling. She would come anytime, day or night. You never knew when she might show up to visit. One night I heard a night nurse outside the door arguing with Mrs. Rawlings, trying to tell her that visiting hours were over. I could hear Mrs. Rawlings talking very loud.

"Say, there is no time limit on me seeing Idella. That's my girl."

After I had been there some time, they all got to know me and I was feeling pretty much at home. The nurses began saying with a laugh, "Idella, here comes your mama."

One day I sensed people all around me, doctors and nurses, everyone hurrying in and out of my room. I heard one of the nurses say, "Idella has a sister out at Florida Normal. We'd better send for her."

I drifted in and out of sleep, and when I woke, Mama was there, wringing her hands and looking very worried. They whispered about an operation and about needing some blood to match mine. My sisters, my mother, all my family lined up to give me blood, but only my sister Eliza and a young man she knew at Florida Normal had a blood type that matched mine. They gave me some blood, but more was needed.

They were all wondering what was to be done when in walked Mrs. Rawlings for one of her visits. She had already had several rounds of drinks, everybody could see that, but as soon as she heard what was going on she said, "Get me ready, test my blood."

Next thing you know, they found out her blood matched mine, and there she was, donating her blood for my operation. You can just imagine my mama's reaction to all this. Her eyes narrowed down and her face tightened up, and she actually told the doctor he was *not* going to put that woman's blood in her child. The doctor pulled her to one side of the room and drew the curtain to talk to her. "This has to be done," he told Mama. "Idella must have blood on hand for this operation, and this woman has blood that matches hers."

Mama was some angry, but at last even she had to admit that it had to be done. She mumbled about the blood being no good, it was mostly whiskey, and so forth, but she kept quiet after that.

Mrs. Rawlings was worried about me, I know, but sometimes I don't think she even knew where she was. She would come in dressed in just anything, sometimes with socks that didn't match. Each time she would keep saying, "You just get well and hurry up and get out of here." She said she didn't have time for me to be sick, and that was true. She had a lot of commitments and things to do.

Mrs. Rawlings gave the doctor orders that I was to stay in the hospital until I was ready to work again, so I stayed there while she made several trips to Cross Creek and out of Florida.

To tell the truth, a good part of all that time in the hospital was recuperating that I could have done at home, but she insisted that I stay. It became almost like a vacation, with my family and Bernard and my other St. Augustine friends coming to visit frequently. When I finally left the hospital, I was completely well and ready to go back to work.

" F I V E "

A Quiet Wedding and a Castle

I hadn't been home from the hospital too many months when Mrs. Rawlings and Mr. Baskin were married. We were back at Cross Creek. She got dressed up all pretty one day in October 1941, and they drove to St. Augustine. She didn't say what she was going to St. Augustine for. When they came back together, she had on a corsage and a big smile.

"Mr. Baskin and I got married today, Idella. From now on you'll have to call me Mrs. Baskin."

I was happy for her, and we hugged one another. She loved him so much, and I know she thought that at last she had the one thing that was going to make her happy. In those early days of the marriage, her life revolved around her new husband. She was happy to go anywhere, do anything he wanted or needed to do. He was still managing the Marion Hotel in Ocala, but soon I heard talk about buying and redecorating a hotel in St. Augustine, and soon it happened.

They bought Castle Warden, a big old stone castle of a hotel right next to the famous Spanish fortress. (Castle Warden has since become Ripley's Believe It or Not Museum, and although a new modern section has been added to the back of the building,

The former Castle Warden Hotel, St. Augustine, now Ripley's Believe It or Not Museum (1990). The windows in the top left corner are part of the penthouse Norton Baskin had redone as an apartment for Marjorie and himself to live in from 1941 to 1942.

the outside still looks just like it did in the forties when Mr. Baskin bought it.)

The top floor was made into a penthouse apartment for Mr. and Mrs. Baskin, but no place for Idella. While the hotel was being readied, they lived mostly at the Crescent Beach cottage, and I lived in my little garage apartment. When they moved into the penthouse, Mrs. Baskin found me a room in a house owned by Mrs. Shaw, a fine black lady who was widowed and owned a large home several blocks from the hotel, in "colored town." I would keep Mrs. Baskin's car and drive over to the hotel each day to see what she needed, but there was little for me to do, really.

Their meals were cooked by the chef in the hotel, Chef Houston. I would get Mrs. Baskin's breakfast tray and take it up to her, and then I would straighten up in the penthouse and see to her clothes. After that, there was nothing to do, so I would go downstairs and sit with the other workers in the kitchen, and sometimes help if I wanted to.

Chef Houston and his wife came with Mr. Baskin to Castle Warden from the Marion Hotel in Ocala. The Houstons' niece, Margie, worked there too, and W. D. Williams was the porter. All these workers came from Ocala. Chef Houston ran the kitchen, loved to yell and shout and curse, and worked his help hard. He kept his kitchen really spotless. Mrs. Houston ran the dining room, and Margie tended to the rooms.

Slowly, the trips to Cross Creek became fewer and farther between, until eventually we were living almost all the time at St. Augustine. Little by little we brought most of Mrs. Rawlings' good things (linens, kitchen utensils, china, decorations, and so on) over to the beach cottage or to Castle Warden. After that, when we did go back to Cross Creek the house seemed different, empty and undressed somehow.

Mrs. Rawlings was in love, I was in love. It never occurred to me that things were bound to change because of her marriage, and I don't think she knew how much things would change either. After all, when you are single you can pick up and go here or there whenever you want. When you're married, you have to ask someone else about it, make plans, and consider the other person as well as yourself. Mrs. Rawlings was used to making up her own mind about where she wanted to be, and of course she had to have peace and solitude to write and work and think. Marriage changed that, too.

After she had been married several months, Mrs. Rawlings

began to be truly restless, as if she was looking for a good quiet place to write, a place far from the noise and excitement of that busy hotel in St. Augustine. Most days we would drive out to the beach cottage.

Many evenings Mr. Baskin would drive down and have dinner with us, sometimes spend the night and let me fix him his favorite, cheese grits, for breakfast. But his first duty was to his hotel. Naturally he was expected to be there, especially in the evenings, greeting and socializing with the guests and seeing that everyone was comfortable.

The way I saw it was this: These two people did the best they could for each other as far as being husband and wife was concerned, in every way. They were very happy when they were together. But Mr. Baskin was a handsome man of the world, who loved people and made his living managing hotels. He had to be dressed up all the time, seeing to the guests' every need and being charming. Mrs. Baskin liked people too, but she also needed solitude to write. She hated being disturbed when she was writing. She disliked being dressed up and loved to be outdoors hunting, fishing, or digging in the soil. Most of all, she loved Cross Creek, and did her best writing there.

But we moved away from Cross Creek, piece by piece, until we were living at St. Augustine, not just staying there part of the time. I am sure this was not the way Mrs. Rawlings planned for it to be, but once she was married, things began to change one way or another.

She would call me and say, "Idella, tomorrow we must go to the Creek for a few days," and her eyes would light up with anticipation. But when we got there, it was not the same place we were both so fond of. We would stay for a day or so, then it would be, "Idella, let's get back to St. Augustine." This moving back and forth went on for a long time. I never knew when we would be going, or where. It began to look to me as if marriage was not the answer to Mrs. Rawlings' problems. She was still restless.

E. M. on Duty

When I found out that Mr. Baskin needed help at Castle Warden, I recommended my brother, Edward Milton Thompson, called "E.M." by everyone, and another friend from Reddick, Leslie Patterson. Both these young men were students at Florida Normal in St. Augustine. Mr. Baskin put Leslie Patterson to work in the kitchen and hired E.M. to be the night doorman and bellhop. They would go to school during the day and work nights.

One night E.M., who was tired out from working day and night, felt too tired to keep his eyes open. It was a quiet night, so he locked the hotel's front door and fell asleep on a couch in the lobby.

Next day Mr. Baskin gave E.M. a serious talking to. He had got a telephone call from a good customer of the hotel. She had come to the hotel late and banged on the door, but it was locked and she got no answer. She was calling him from another hotel. Mr. Baskin gave E.M. a stern lecture about always leaving the hotel doors open.

E.M. worked there for most of two school terms, and then he and Leslie Patterson bought a broken-down old Ford and set out on a trip to New York. World War II had started, and both men knew they were sure to be drafted soon. They were determined to have one last good time before Uncle Sam called them up.

I told E.M. he should go home and see Mama before he left for New York, but he had his own reasoning about the trip. He wanted to be in New York when he was drafted.

"Miss Della," he said to me, "Uncle Sam will give me leave to go home and see Mama, but he won't give me leave to go to New York. I mean to see New York before I go."

So he and Leslie set out in that wreck of a car, and it took over a week to get to New York, because the car kept breaking down, but they made it.

Soon after, E.M. was drafted. He did have two furloughs, and he came to Reddick to see Mama before he left to fight. On the

My brother, Edward Milton Thompson (called "E. M."), in 1944, just before he was killed in action in World War II.

first trip home, he got married, and when we received word that he had been killed in action, there was a baby on the way. He knew about the baby from letters, and asked her to be named Joyce Ann, but he never got to see her.

My boyfriend, Bernard Young, was a real charmer. All the women admired him, so why shouldn't I? He was handsome, he was always dressed so sporty, and laughed and flashed those beautiful teeth. He made me feel good.

When I was living at Mrs. Shaw's in St. Augustine he would come calling on me, and he took care to act like a fine gentleman. Mrs. Shaw was such a respectable, fine, upstanding woman, so admired in the black community, that when Bernard sat in her parlor, he sat up straight. Mrs. Shaw intimidated Bernard, so he always had a plan for us to go out somewhere. Ball games, the drugstore–ice cream parlor, a good movie, a card party, always somewhere, so he could get me out from under the watchful eye of Mrs. Shaw. All this social life was a welcome change for me, after those lonesome years at Cross Creek.

One day I drove a group of friends, including Bernard, to Tampa for a ball game, and on the way back we stopped in Reddick to say hello to my family. I was so proud to introduce my handsome, charming boyfriend to Mama. Mama took one look and called me into the kitchen. She looked me straight in the eye and said, "Della, that man is no good. Let him alone."

This hurt me. I was upset with Mama, and we made our visit very short that day. I couldn't understand why Mama took such a quick dislike to Bernard, without getting to know him like I did. Surely she would change her mind after she got to know him. It never occurred to me that Mama might be right.

To make a long story short, Bernard and I were married. He said that he would take care of me, and that I wouldn't have to work for "that old woman" any more, and his promises sounded wonderful to me. Not have to work, after so many years of back-breaking labor in other people's houses? It sounded like heaven to me.

So I went and told Mrs. Rawlings that Bernard and I were married and I wouldn't be working for her any more. She went into a terrible flurry over this. What was she going to do without me, couldn't we work something out, there must be some way I could still work for her and be married, too. But I was firm, and stuck to my plan to move in with Bernard and his mother, and be like a mother to his two little children. Mrs. Rawlings was very upset, but she wished me all the best.

For a short time everything was ideal. Bernard was working in one of the busiest barber shops in St. Augustine and making good money. I was caring for the children and keeping house, and his mother, "Mrs. Johnny," was not hard to get along with. For once I was free. I felt like the old Negro anthem, "Free at last, free at last." I didn't have to go to a job, I could go to the church of my choice, and I had a tall, handsome husband to look after me. I was out of the woods and living in a nice city with all the comforts. I put Mrs. Rawlings and her problems out of my mind and concentrated on being a newlywed. I was truly happy!

But Bernard was not like me and my family. He was one of these who didn't really want to work hard to get what he wanted, and he was not dependable.

One day soon after we married, he called from the barbershop and told me to get the children ready and we would all go out to a movie. I did as he asked, and when the time came the children and I sat down on the front porch to wait for Bernard. Hours passed, no Bernard. The children fell asleep on the porch, and I put them to bed. Midnight came, no Bernard. Finally, about two in the morning, here comes Bernard, heels clicking on the sidewalk, whistling as he walked. When he came into the bedroom, I asked him where he'd been. "Out," he said, and started to get undressed like nothing had happened. There was a big fight that night, and before it was over, Bernard needed gold caps on his teeth.

I was ready to leave Bernard and go home to Mama that very night. I wrote to my sister Thelma about the problems I was having with Bernard, and instead of sympathy she wrote back and said that I should be *made* to stay with him, because I should have listened to Mama in the first place. I stuck it out and stayed with Bernard for seven long years, but it was never an ideal marriage. Knowing that I could never depend on Bernard, I went back to work for Mrs. Rawlings only a few weeks after I married him.

Mr. Baskin Gives Bernard a Job

Mr. Baskin enlisted in the army during the last years of World War II. While he was away, he and Mrs. Baskin wrote back and forth every day. Sometimes she would not hear from him, and she would worry. Finally he was taken sick and they flew him home to recuperate. Mrs. Rawlings flew up to New York to meet him, and eventually they came home.

Mrs. Baskin had a lot of fan mail coming in during the war, especially from soldiers, and she tried to answer every single letter. Her writing took second place to these letters, I think, and seemed to be off schedule more than it was on.

When Mr. Baskin came back, he sold Castle Warden and became manager of the restaurant and bar on the beach at Marineland, about fifteen miles south of St. Augustine. Many of the Castle Warden employees, like Mr. and Mrs. Houston, came to Marineland with Mr. Baskin. But W. D. Williams, who had been the porter at Castle Warden, left for New York, and Mr. Baskin had an opening for a bartender and driver.

Mrs. Baskin came to see me one day and said that Mr. Baskin would give Bernard a good job at Marineland, and I could come back and work for her at the cottage. We could live in the garage apartment. Bernard liked the idea of free rent and food, for we would both eat our meals on the job, and so we took the offer.

Every morning Bernard would drive to St. Augustine in one of the Marineland jeeps and pick up Mr. Baskin's workers and drive them to Marineland. This part of the job was a disaster because Bernard kept flipping these jeeps over, I guess by driving too fast and hitting the sandy shoulders of the road. I don't know *how* many of these jeeps Bernard tore up. Mr. Baskin would call

Bernard in and talk to him about these accidents, and Bernard would promise to be more careful.

On days when I had Mrs. Baskin's car, she would always tell me not to let Bernard drive. So I would drive, but as soon as we were out of sight of the cottage and around the first bend, Bernard would make me stop and let him drive. Bernard always had his way where I was concerned.

Finally, there was one too many jeeps wrecked, and Bernard was fired. He was mad as could be with Mr. Baskin, and cussed a blue streak about being fired. He tried his best to talk me into quitting Mrs. Baskin, but for once I put my foot down and refused to leave. He went back to the barbershop to work, but we were still married and we still lived at Crescent Beach.

From the time Bernard lost the job at Marineland, he kept trying to get me to quit Mrs. Baskin and come back to town to live with him. We argued back and forth about this for more than a year.

Bernard and the Rattlesnake

Mr. and Mrs. Baskin had little use for Bernard, but they put up with him because he was my husband. One day I realized just how little love Mr. Baskin had for him.

I was at the cottage, working. Mrs. Baskin had gone into town to do some errands, and Mr. Baskin was in the cottage, resting. I went down to the garage apartment, and there outside my door, slithering toward the oleander hedges, was one of the biggest rattlesnakes I had ever seen. I skirted around him and ran into my room to get the double-barrel shotgun I had there. I loaded up and came back out, took careful aim, and blasted the snake.

"I got him, I got him," I yelled, loud as I could. Mr. Baskin came running out of the house and leaned over the rail.

"Idella, what's the matter?"

"I got him, Mr. Baskin, I shot a snake."

"Oh hell, Idella," said Mr. Baskin. He turned away, and there was real disappointment in his voice. "I thought it was Bernard you shot!"

The Roadside Restaurant

Among Mr. and Mrs. Baskin's best friends in St. Augustine were Mr. and Mrs. Owen Young. The two couples often had dinner and played bridge together. The Youngs were very wealthy from what I could tell, and they had several houses, one of which was in Van Hornesville, New York, a little town west of Albany, not far from Cooperstown. I think it must have been Mrs. Young who told Mrs. Baskin what a pretty town it was, and how nice and cool and quiet it would be up there so that she could write. So plans were made, and in June of 1947 we were off to Van Hornesville.

Mr. Baskin drove us up, planning to get us settled, stay for a couple of weeks, and then go back to Florida by himself. What a trip! Husband and wife in the front seat, Idella in the back seat with Uki, the Siamese cat, a happy, drooling dog named Moe, and a pile of luggage.

We left Florida early in the morning, and toward noon we were beginning to be hot, tired, and hungry for some lunch. We must have been in Georgia, maybe even South Carolina by then.

By and by the Baskins caught sight of a small roadside restaurant, and we pulled into the dusty driveway. It was not a fancy place at all, just a plain box of a building, in need of some paint, with a few rusty tin Coca-Cola signs tacked to the outside. They got out and walked in, and Moe raced in the door with them. I brought up the rear, after making sure that Uki was safely locked up in the car.

By the time I got to the door, I could hear Mrs. Baskin asking the man at the front counter if we could all wash up and use the restroom before we sat down to eat. Moe was sniffing around the tables, inspecting the premises, and the manager didn't seem to mind the dog.

There were flies buzzing in the air, and a few customers sat at tables covered with red checkered oilcloth, some eating, others fanning themselves with their menus, waiting for their orders, all talking.

As the screen door slammed shut behind me, the place suddenly got very quiet, like the sound had been turned off at a movie. All eyes turned toward me. The manager, who had just been telling Mrs. Baskin where the bathrooms were, looked directly at me and said, "You all can use them, but not that nigger."

I saw Mrs. Baskin stiffen and pull herself up straighter. She wheeled around, and I could see that her face was red and her eyes were narrowed down to little angry slits.

"Come on, Norton," she said loudly. "We're not staying if Idella can't." And she stomped out the door and kept right on stomping to the car. Mr. Baskin came running out behind her. "But Margie," he pleaded, "I've got to go to the bathroom." Mrs. Baskin paid no attention. She called Moe to get in the car, I climbed in with him, and she got in, too.

"Let's go," she demanded, and reluctantly he did what she said.

Down the road several miles he pulled the car over in a deserted stretch of woods, and we took turns going behind the trees.

Summer in Van Hornesville

The first house we stayed in belonged to Mrs. Young, and Mrs. Young's gardener helped us tend the yard and garden. It was a nice old cottage, but there was a lot of work to be done before it was in livable condition. It was set on a narrow, winding road and looked out across a valley to a beautiful mountain.

Just as we arrived at Mr. and Mrs. Young's house, Mrs. Baskin received word of the sudden death of her editor and friend, Max Perkins. His death shocked her very much, and she just could

Postcard depicting a bird's-eye view of Van Hornesville, New York, in the 1940s.

not seem to get over it. She would walk through the house, wringing her hands and crying, "Now what am I going to do?" She would go off in the woods on long walks, walk the floors for hours, smoking and drinking, calling out his name. She could not seem to settle down to her work, and her writing just fell off.

However, Van Hornesville turned out to be everything Mrs. Young had promised, and Mrs. Baskin liked it so well that she bought a house there during that summer of 1947. It had to be restored, and it wasn't ready for her to move in until the following year.

"Do More Than Fifty Dollars' Worth"

For me the summer was lonely, being in a new place. I passed the time reading, crocheting, and walking. Mrs. Baskin gave me Thursdays off, and I would take rides in the countryside around Van Hornesville, enjoying the farms and watching the workers in the fields, or sometimes I would drive the ten miles to Cooperstown for a movie or some window-shopping.

One Thursday I went to visit the Baseball Hall of Fame, and there I met a group of young black men and women my own age who were working for some families from Albany. Pretty soon we were going out together and enjoying visits back and forth on our days off.

One day the gang suggested that we drive to Albany to see a baseball game. This sounded like great fun to me, so I said, "Let's go," and off we went. One of the young men in the group asked me if he could drive, and here I made a big mistake. I let him drive Mrs. Baskin's car. I should not have done that, because I had no idea what his driving ability was, and I was soon to regret it.

We never did get to that game. We had dinner in Albany and rode around sight-seeing, and then it happened. He ran right into the side of another car. I was fit to die. The police came and asked for the registration and asked the questions they always ask. I was quite lucky that evening, for the policeman let me call Mrs. Baskin.

I don't even know what I said to her, but I remember her yelling at me, "Idella, let me speak to that policeman." I don't know what she said to him, but when he got off the phone, we were told to go on home.

The next day we had to drive back to the police station in Albany to get things settled, and Mrs. Baskin was upset, because she had work to do. To my surprise, she never found out that I was not driving the car.

I was scared to face her, but believe it or not, the only thing she said about the accident was "Idella, next time you have a wreck, for God's sake do more than fifty dollars' worth of damage, so the insurance will pay for it."

Back to Van Hornesville

In the spring of 1948 we returned to Van Hornesville, this time without Mr. Baskin. On the trip north, Mrs. Baskin and I took turns driving. It was my turn to drive, and we were just leaving Virginia when a big semi truck passed us.

Mrs. Baskin looked up at it and said, "Now, Idella, just stay behind that truck. He's going straight into New York City."

I wondered how she knew that, because the truck had several different state tags on it, but as usual I followed her orders. I had no need to look for further road signs, all I had to do was follow the truck, which I did. We were supposed to be in New York City that night, but when the truck finally stopped, we were in Youngstown, Ohio.

You should have heard the yelling and carrying on that Mrs. Baskin did: "My God, now I've got to find some place for us to stay." This was not an easy job, as our party included a white woman, two cats, a big dog, and a black maid. By and by she did find a shabby place, one of those old roadside motels. Of course we had to sneak the animals in with her, and I was in a room on the other side of the motel altogether. Next morning we set off again for Van Hornesville.

Uki Up an Apple Tree

Soon after we arrived, we set to work making a little garden at the new house. The soil was dark and rich, not at all like the sandy Florida soil, and everything had to be planted in high beds so that water would run off the plants.

There were apple orchards all around, and they were lovely. I had never seen apple trees before, and I was enchanted with them. You could hardly walk among the trees, the ground was covered with so many fallen apples. There were all types of apples, large and small. The only apples I had ever seen were in food stores and we had to buy them. My family could not buy many, and I can remember many Christmases we got one apple in our stockings and thought it was a wonderful treat. You can understand how excited I was when first I saw those apple orchards.

I thought that I would eat my poor self to death, but finally I caught up with the eating. Mrs. Baskin and I made every kind of apple dessert you could name: sauces, jelly, cobbler, candied, baked. Oh, it was such fun, and it made the weeks pass quickly.

When I think of the apple trees, I think of Uki, Mrs. Baskin's Siamese cat.

One night, very late, Mrs. Baskin woke me and said, "Idella, Uki's gone. He didn't come in. Come help me find him."

I got up and put on a robe, not very cheerful after being roused out of a sound sleep over a cat.

We both took flashlights and walked out among the trees for the better part of an hour, calling "Come, Uki," over and over. Finally, there comes a little "meow, meow" from high up in a tree. We shone our flashlights up, and there in the highest branches sat Uki, glaring down at us, as if to say, "Don't they know I can get down whenever I want to?"

All of a sudden, he turned around and ran straight down the tree, jumped to the ground, and started rubbing all over Mrs. Baskin's legs. She picked him up and hugged him under her chin, saying, "Now, baby, don't do that again."

By the time we got back we were covered with dirt and scratches we got struggling through the woods looking for that fool cat. I stomped back to bed, upset with having to be called out of my bed to go out in the woods and look for a cat who all of us knew would come when he was ready.

Mrs. Baskin's Yankee House

The new house was a pretty, pretty two-story white house, set on a narrow, winding mountain road away from everything. There were no other houses close by, at least none in sight.

I believe this house had several parts built onto the main house. My room and bath and the garage, which were all on the east side, were two steps down from the kitchen and the main part of the house. All the other bedrooms were upstairs, far away from mine. These houses in Van Hornesville were the first ones in which my quarters were under the same roof as Mrs. Baskin's.

In the yard and the meadows around the house there were deer, some running, some grazing, others standing still. Some would run when they saw you, others would just stand still. To see these beautiful brown creatures poised, ready to run, against that beautiful, green, smoky mountain certainly was a beautiful sight. I watched them every morning from my kitchen window.

The deer were one of the few lovely things I remember about that second summer. Most of the other memories are painful ones for me.

The friends I had made the summer before did not come back, so I did not have any black friends at all, and it was very lonesome. While Mrs. Baskin and I were in Van Hornesville, our husbands stayed behind to work in Florida. After driving us up, Mr. Baskin had gone back to run the restaurant at Marineland. Bernard was back and forth between our little apartment at the beach cottage and his mother's house in St. Augustine. He was not working for Mr. Baskin any more, and he had nothing good to say about "that old lady" I was working for. He wrote letters, urging me to come home and leave her, he would take care of me. In light of the way Mrs. Baskin was drinking, Bernard's letters made good sense.

When she drank too much, she could be unreasonable. I recall her telephoning Mr. Baskin, insisting that he come to Van Hornesville right away. She wanted him to be there right then, and she could not seem to understand that he was thousands of miles away and could not be there right away. He had a business to run, and it must have been hard for him to drop everything and run to Van Hornesville, but several days later, he arrived. I had the impression that it was not a happy visit, and he only stayed a few days. They took long walks together in the woods, and their faces were stormy when they came back.

I protected Mrs. Baskin from others as much as possible. Many times I had to tell untruths, to protect her. I am thinking about a night in Van Hornesville when she and her guests, Mr. and Mrs. Owen Young and a friend of theirs, were having dinner. During the main course Mrs. Baskin, who had had quite a lot to drink, jumped up from the table and hurried up to her room without saying anything.

After a while we heard a heavy thump on the floor above us. I said, "Let me go up and see about her."

I went upstairs and opened the door. She had completely undressed and was stretched out on the floor, naked. My heart went out to her.

"Oh, Mrs. Baskin," I said. As I opened the door, she grabbed the covers from the bed and put them around her. Then she sat up and looked at me and said, "Don't you tell them."

I went back to the dining room and said, "She doesn't feel well." I served the dessert, and the guests finished dinner and left. As they were leaving, Mrs. Young pulled me aside and whispered, "Now you take care of her, Idella."

At breakfast the next day Mrs. Baskin acted as if nothing unusual had happened. But later in the day she asked me, "How did I behave last night, Idella? Tell me about it." I told her the truth, and all she said was, "Oh, my God." She looked embarrassed. This scene was repeated too many times to suit my liking, most often when Mr. Baskin was away and there was no one but me to see to her.

Many, many times the next day she would ask, "Idella, how did I act last night?" or "When did they leave? What did they say?", sometimes with a slight smile. She would cross her legs and blow on her cigarette. I felt sorry for her and wished there was something I could do to help. Often she would promise never to do it again, but the promises were not kept.

In the midst of all this turmoil, I took a few days off to visit a cousin of mine and some other Florida friends who lived in Brooklyn. I took the train to New York, and that's where I was when I got a telegram from Reddick telling me that my dear grandfather, Papa Jake, had died.

Now I was faced with a dilemma. I had no clothes or money with me for a trip to Florida, and if I took the train back to Van Hornesville to pack and then started on the train trip to Florida, I would not make it in time for the funeral. Much as I wanted to go, I did not see how I could do it, so I sent flowers and wired my family that I would not be able to be there.

Meanwhile, Bernard took the bus from St. Augustine to Reddick and went to Papa Jake's funeral. He was very put out when he learned that I was not going to be there. I'm sure he thought that if he could meet me at the funeral he could talk me out of going back to Van Hornesville and into coming to St. Augustine with him.

The next week I got a letter from Bernard. He tried to make me feel ashamed that I had not been at the funeral. He, after all, had closed his barbershop for the day out of respect for Papa Jake and had gone to the funeral, and he wasn't even related to the man. I was family, blood-related. Why wasn't I there?

He closed with the usual demand: "When are you coming home?" But this time he added a new threat: "It's going to be me or that woman. You make your choice." He told me he had decided to move to New York City and stay with his brother until he could set up a barbershop, and he said I could come, or not.

I was torn between being with my husband and trying to please Mrs. Baskin and stay with her because I knew she needed me. A few weeks later, Bernard wrote again, this time from New York. He was staying with his brother, Jimmy, in Brooklyn. There was plenty of work in New York, he said, no need to stay with that old woman. But I stayed on with Mrs. Baskin, and drove back down to Florida in the fall with her.

We wrote back and forth all that fall and winter. Bernard's letters were always along the same lines. When are you going to leave that old woman? Come to New York, we'll be happy. She can't make you happy; I can.

What Could I Do?

Bernard was right about one thing; Mrs. Baskin could not make me happy. Just the opposite. Her demands on me were enormous. I'm not talking about work, now, I'm talking about emotional demands.

As a writer, she needed peace and quiet and to be away from her husband. We all understood this, and although long separations might not have suited other couples, the Baskins did not seem bothered.

However, when Mr. Baskin was away, Mrs. Baskin had no one else to lean on but me. She would go through depressions and bouts of sickness, dark moods and terrible drinking sprees, and here was Idella, trying to cope with her day and night.

In time, I could tell from the look of Mrs. Baskin's face or her tone of voice when she needed me. At times we would hug and cry together when there was nothing else to be done. These times when she would cling to me, sobbing out all her fears and anxieties, were the times that were hardest for me. She told me things I am sure she would never have told anyone else, and leaned on me in ways that few people ever knew. I have often told Mr. Baskin that I know more about Mrs. Rawlings than anyone, and I know that's the truth, because she held nothing back in her times of need.

She was a good, kind woman who never meant anyone any harm. The person she hurt the most was herself. Our relationship was a close one, but it was one that often felt burdensome to me. Still, I did my best to protect her and help her. I loved her then, and I love her still, but what could I do?

A person gets weary carrying another person's misery and woe, and gradually I was beginning to feel that I could not carry Mrs. Baskin's much longer.

Breaking Free

Bernard came down to Florida for Christmas in 1949, because he knew that I would be there with my family. He stayed a few weeks, and before he went back to New York he told me again, "You do what you want."

I stayed in Florida, and I tossed back and forth all the rest of the winter. We kept writing to one another, and gradually I made up my mind to leave Mrs. Baskin and go to New York to be with my husband.

By spring I had made up my mind, but I was afraid to tell Mrs. Baskin. I knew she would try to make me stay, and she could be very strong and determined when she wanted things to be her way. I did not want to have any arguments or unpleasant scenes, and the right moment to tell her never seemed to come, so I said nothing.

We packed as usual for the trip north to Van Hornesville, but instead of packing my things the way I usually did, I was bundling up my belongings and taking them to Mama's house. Mr. Baskin decided that he would drive Mrs. Baskin and the animals to New York that year, and they arranged for me to travel by bus. I was to stay at Mama's for a week or so, then take the bus to New York and visit Bernard for a week, and then go up to Van Hornesville.

They took me to the bus station in St. Augustine, and I can see her now, standing by the bus, waving to me and calling, "Now, Idella, you contact me and let me know when you're coming!"

As the bus pulled out, she waved and smiled, and that's the last time I ever saw Marjorie Rawlings.

I wrote to Mrs. Baskin from New York and told her that I would be staying with Bernard, and that I would no longer be working for her. It was hard for me to write that letter after so many years together. Hard for me, and hard for her. But it had to be done.

She wrote back immediately, wanting to know how I could do this to her. This letter was followed by two or three others, and I never answered any of them. There was nothing more to say.

Bernard and I got a little one-bedroom apartment in his brother's house in Brooklyn, and we took a job on Long Island working as a couple for a lovely Jewish family. I did the cooking, and Bernard waited on table and did the driving. Bernard was neat and good-looking, but he was no more dependable than he was when I first met him. Eventually we lost the job because of Bernard, and we came back to the city.

His many letters begging me to leave Mrs. Baskin and join him made me think that Bernard had changed for the better, but I was wrong. He was just as mean to me as ever, and things had not improved a bit. Within a year I left him. I got myself a little room on the other side of Brooklyn and rented a booth in a nice beauty salon and began doing hair.

I was there a couple of months before Bernard located me and tried to wheedle his way back into my life. He knew I would be going to Mama's for Christmas, so he tried to get my favor by offering to see me off at the train at Penn Station. As the train pulled out he gave me his most beautiful smile and held up two fingers.

"I'll see you in two weeks," he said, and I held my breath, hoping the train would pull out before he had a chance to pull me off of it. At last the door closed, and I felt a great wave of relief sweep over me.

From Florida I wrote to Bernard that I would not be coming back. The marriage is over, I told him, and the next time you hear from me will be through my lawyer. Bernard was so mad when he got that letter that he wrote back (on a little scrap of paper that must have been all he could find in his hurry): "Idella, you are lower than a snake."

And that was the end of Bernard and Idella.

Within the space of just a few years I had stood up to two very strong people I loved and told them *no more*. I shook off the ties that bound me to both Mrs. Rawlings and Bernard and refused to be used and emotionally drained by either of them any longer. In both cases it took me a long time to come around to speaking up for myself and declaring my independence from them.

People who know me now find me outspoken and quick to speak up when I see wrong being done. In fact, sometimes I'm called just plain ornery. I know they will be surprised to read that I was quiet and obedient, as all colored girls were supposed to be in those days, and endured so many unhappy years before throwing off the chains that bound me.

When I think back on the tumultuous years I spent with Mrs. Baskin and the misery with Bernard, it reminds me in a way of slavery, the way I was supposed to take whatever hardship and abuse was served to me and say nothing. Finally I rebelled, just as the slaves did, and I sometimes wonder if that's not the Turner blood in me. Uncle Adam Turner was over a hundred years old when he died in 1929, as determined and independent a man as I have ever known. If my newfound independence and determination to be my own person had anything to do with his blood, I thank him for it.

A Last Word from Mrs. Baskin

In 1953 I had a last letter from Mrs. Baskin. She mentioned that she had never found a maid who could replace me.

"Idella, come to Cross Creek," she wrote, "and let's see if we can't get things straightened out." She set a date and a time.

I did not answer the letter, and I did not jump to go where and when she told me to. By this time I had met and married my second husband, I had a nice life, and I knew I could not let myself get tangled up with her again.

Weeks later I was shocked to hear from a friend that Mrs. Baskin had died suddenly, and had been buried in Island Grove. I felt great sadness at her passing, and regretted that things had not been different in those last years we had been together.

Marjorie Kinnan Rawlings Baskin was a remarkable woman, full of contrasts. She was a strong woman, but she had many weaknesses. She was a very independent woman, but she loved to have things done for her. She was known for her wit, yet she seldom smiled. She cared deeply for others and very little about her own comfort, yet she could also be thoughtless. She loved to write and create books, but each one was difficult and took an enormous toll on her.

In many ways she was ahead of her time, especially in her attitude toward race relations. Yet she could not bring herself to allow a person of color to sleep in her home, and she often called us "niggers" when speaking or writing to other white people.

To me she was two different people, kind and generous one moment, and before the day was over cursing and yelling at me for one thing or another. When she felt that she had hurt me she would always come hugging, apologizing, promising not to do it again. She would buy me something or volunteer to make breakfast. "I'm making up for yesterday," she'd say. "Take the car to Wilson's and buy yourself a hat."

When I learned of her death, I spent many hours recalling our years together, and found that I missed her very much, and still do.

Bus Parker

I met Samuel Parker, called "Bus" by everyone who knew him, in 1950, not very long after I left Bernard. Soon after we met, we became involved. Bus worked as a shoemaker in Ocala, and he was divorced. Ours was a short courtship, held mostly on Wednesdays, when his shop was closed, and on Sundays when I

My second husband, Bus Parker, with my sister Dorothy (c. 1952).

would see him in church. Bus knew what he wanted and set out
to get it.

One day he asked me, right out, "Will you marry me?"

"Well, I can't," I said. "I'm still married to Bernard."

"I didn't ask you if you were married," said Bus. "I asked you
if you would marry me." This was his way of telling me that he
would see that I got the divorce, and he did.

Soon after that he said, "Go look for a house."

Again I hesitated: "I can't afford a house."

"I didn't ask you if you could afford a house. I said go look for
a house."

And again he smoothed everything out. I found a nice home
in Reddick, just being put up for sale. Bus bought the house, and
we were married in it. I had a beauty shop there at the house, and

he had a shoe shop. I had eight happy years with Bus Parker before he became ill and died of a liver ailment.

Life Goes On

Two years after Bus's death, Mama died. She was sitting in her rocking chair on her big screened porch and had asked my sister Thelma to go look for something. When Thelma came back, Mama had fallen asleep in the chair, never to waken.

These two deaths were very hard for me to bear, and my younger sister Eliza sensed that I needed a change. She invited me to come and spend some time with her in Pompano Beach, and I went gladly.

The day I arrived, Eliza went to get her hair done. When she came back, she told me that her hairdresser was going into the hospital for an operation and needed a senior operator to take her place. I slipped into that job and made many friends in just a short time. There was really no reason to go back home to Reddick, so I stayed, rented a booth, and settled into life there.

In 1965 I met a white beautician named Marie, and we started talking about what might happen when integration came, as it was surely coming. She suggested that I come work with her. She knew that I could do white hair, and she wanted me to show her how to do black hair, and together we could do both. I went to work with her in Fort Lauderdale and rented a small house to live in.

One day the landlady who owned my house stopped by to collect her rent. I had just made a cake, and I offered her a piece, never suspecting that she was supervisor of home economics for the Broward County School Department.

"Mrs. Parker, is this made from scratch?" she asked.

"Scratch?" I pretended to be outraged. "What you mean, scratch? Everything I make is from scratch." I ran to get my autographed copy of *Cross Creek Cookery* and show her that I was the Idella mentioned in that book.

She immediately invited me to come to Dillard High School and talk to the girls about homemaking skills. That first visit eventually led to my becoming a teacher of vocational home-making to educable mentally retarded (EMR) students at the Melrose Park Center in Fort Lauderdale, and to single welfare mothers at the Opportunity Center in Pompano Beach. I retired from teaching in 1976.

Full Circle

After retirement, I returned to Reddick and later sold my house and moved to Ocala. My father, who was living with my sister Dorothy, became ill, and I needed to be near to help with his care. This I did until his death in 1990.

Papa was blind for the last ten years of his life, and the five of us girls took turns caring for him. Sometimes he went to stay with Hettie in Jacksonville, sometimes to Pompano Beach to spend time with Eliza. Many times Thelma and her husband, Alva, would take Papa for rides around Reddick and describe the various sights to him. He lived a very useful life and became the town's unofficial living historian. People often came to visit him and make tapes of what he told them about Reddick.

Mr. Camp Again!

One day in 1988 I stopped by to see my old friend Berylene Hooker, a hairdresser and now a city councilwoman in Reddick.

"Idella, there is a man I know from Ocala who comes in to get his hair cut. He's been sick, and he needs some help. His name is Bob Camp."

"Bob Camp!" I cried. "Well, for pete's sake, I know Bob Camp. I talked to him about a job once. His mother is the person I was looking for when Mrs. Rawlings came and gave me that first check."

I called him right away, and we had a joyful time talking about

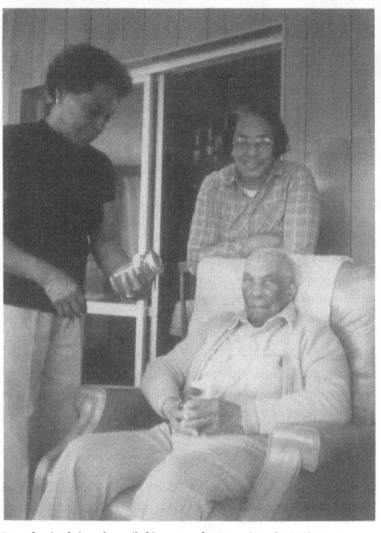

Dorothy (right) and me (left), caring for Papa (April 1983).

the old days. For the next two years I worked for Mr. Camp off and on, and we remained good friends, keeping in touch by telephone and with short visits.

Mr. Camp's health began to decline badly in 1990, but he never tired of talking about the old days "with Norton and Marjorie." When I spoke to him late in July 1991, he said to me, "Idella, I sure hope to read your book. How is it coming?" I told him all about it, but I could tell that he was becoming tired. I told him to rest and not talk, and he said, "Idella, I wish you could come over and broil me a lamb chop."

Those were his last words to me, for Bob Camp passed away on August 15, 1991.

Mr. Camp was well known locally as an artist. Perhaps you have seen some of his sketches in *Cross Creek Cookery*. I noticed that one of his paintings was hanging over the fireplace in the house at Cross Creek. The guides at the house had no idea who had painted it, but I did, and told them it was Bob Camp's work. They invited Mr. Camp to the house one day and he signed the painting, so now everyone knows who painted it.

In those early days at Cross Creek Mr. Camp was a frequent visitor, a friend Mrs. Rawlings could always count on. In one of our last chats Mr. Camp told me that she called on him to drive her to Tampa for a last visit with Charles Rawlings before their divorce was final. Of course, that was before I knew her.

His mother, the lady I might have been working for if Mrs. Rawlings had not gotten me first, was always put out that Marjorie Rawlings had stolen me from her. She politely refused most of Mrs. Rawlings' dinner invitations, but I do recall she came to the Creek once. I could hear her coming long before she got to the kitchen.

"Where's this Idella? I have to meet this Idella I've been hearing about!"

She was an elegant woman, the kind who looked like she never set foot in a kitchen in her life, and she was very nice. She chatted for a minute about how I really should have been working for her, and asked about the various dishes I was preparing for dinner.

As I think about Mrs. Camp's visit, and the mistake which led to my working for Mrs. Rawlings, I wonder how different my life might have been if I had worked for Mrs. Camp. But there's no

I revisit the Crescent Beach cottage (1990).

I celebrate my seventy-seventh birthday at Cross Creek.

In the kitchen at
Cross Creek (1978).

I show Cross Creek historian Sally Morrison how Marjorie Kinnan
Rawlings styled her hair (1978).

My grandfather, "Papa Jake," my sister Eliza, and me in front of Hettie's house in Jacksonville, Florida (1944). This photo was taken on the only trip Papa Jake ever took away from his hometown of Reddick, Florida.

Hettie, Mama, and me with Joyce Ann, the daughter E.M. never saw, in front of Papa and Mama's house in Reddick (1951).

Papa and Mama in their living room in Reddick, Florida (1960).

Papa and his five daughters at Thelma's house in Reddick, Florida (c. 1980).

All of Papa's granddaughters with their husbands at Papa's ninetieth birthday party (1987).

My nieces (c. 1979), left to right: Iatrice, Gail, Marcia, and Gwen.

Papa, age 96, with his great-grandchildren (1986).

sense wondering about such things. After all, the good Lord has a plan for each of us, and his plan for me must have been to be Marjorie Rawlings' "perfect maid." Good times and bad weighed together, I wouldn't trade the experience for any other.

Will *There Be Any Stars in My Crown?*

In Reddick, the place where I was born and grew up, the place where I still feel the ties of home, there is an old story told. I guess you could call it a local legend, for it has come down many generations and is still told there.

Southeast of the center of town, across the railroad tracks, there were four or five tiny little three-room shacks known as the Sexton houses. These were places where less fortunate families, colored and white, lived. Many of the men who lived in these poor hovels worked for the railroad.

127

One day, as the story goes, there was a jet-black woman doing her week's laundry in an old tin washtub outside her tiny house. As she rubbed those clothes on the washboard, tired from the work of keeping her house and tending her children, thinking of the work yet to be done after the clothes were hung out to dry, weary to her bones from the hard work of living, she began to sing.

Her song was one she learned from her mother, and it began deep down inside her, low and sweet, and rose in the morning air, clear and beautiful. "Will there be any stars in my crown?" she sang, and her rich black voice soared over the poor houses and up into heaven itself.

On the porch of the house next door sat a poor white woman, rocking a tiny baby in her arms. The woman's arms were burned and freckled from working in the hot sun, and her hair fell limp and lifeless around her dull blue eyes. The baby, wrapped in little more than rags, fretted and fussed in her arms.

"Will there be any stars in my crown?" sang the glorious black voice.

The white woman lifted her head and sang the reply in her loud, thin voice, "No, not one. No, not one."

It is said that the poor colored woman ran into her house, very sad and shedding tears, unable to say anything to the white woman.

When I think back over the years I spent with Mrs. Rawlings, I know that there was something of this story in our relationship, too. Our friendship was an unusually close one for the times we lived in. Yet no matter what the ties were that bound us together, we were still a black woman and a white woman, and the barrier of race was always there.

In private, we were often like sisters, laughing and chatting and enjoying one another's company. We shared many years together, helped one another through bad times, and rejoiced for each other's happiness. Between the two of us there was deep friendship and respect, and no thought of the social differences between us.

But whenever other people were around, the barrier of color went up automatically. Without acknowledging that we were doing so, we became more distant to one another. She became the rich, white lady author, and I became quiet, reserved, and slipped back into her shadow, "the perfect maid."

INDEX